Thank
You!!!

[signature]

C.E.O.

Romans
8:17

THE **6**
INDICATORS
FOR BUSINESS & LIFE

KELLY CARDENAS

emerge
publishing

TULSA, OKLAHOMA

23 22 21 20 19 18   8 7 6 5 4 3 2 1

The Six Indicators for Business and Life–
©2018 Kelly Cardenas

TULSA. OKLAHOMA

Published by:
Emerge Publishing, LLC
9521B Riverside Parkway, Suite 243
Tulsa, Oklahoma 74137
Phone: 888.407.4447
www.EmergePublishing.com

Library of Congress Cataloging-in-Publication Data

ISBN: 978-1-943127-80-1   Hardcover
         978-1-943127-81-8   E-book

BISAC Category:
BUS020000   BUSINESS & ECONOMICS / Business Development
BUS025000   BUSINESS & ECONOMICS / Entrepreneurship
SEL027000   SELF-HELP / Personal Growth / Success

Printed in the United States of America.

TABLE OF CONTENTS

DEDICATION

I would like to dedicate this book to my beautiful
wife, Brooklyn, my loving daughter Makena
and my superhero of a son, Maddox.

"Kelly first told me about the six indicators three and a half years ago. My first response to Kelly was "are you writhing a book on this? Because the information is mind blowing." Not only does Kelly's Six Business Indicators work within the salon environment, but in all types of business. If you don't have a way to measure your business, you will never know where and how fast your going. Kelly and his business principles have changed my outlook on life for the better. Read his book! You won't be disappointed!"

Amanda Moncur
Stylist
Kelly Cardenas Salon

"I have had the honor and pleasure of working with Kelly. He has taught me his 6 Indicators and it has now become a part of my everyday life. There is no doubt that Kelly's 6 Indicators have helped me to build my Business and become successful. But more than that, it has taught me to expand my mindset to what is possible. I am so grateful to have the 6 Indicators in my life and would absolutely recommend it to anyone in any business."

Taylor Nawyn
Stylist
Kelly Cardenas Salon

"If you've ever met Kelly Cardenas, you won't believe he sat still long enough to write a book! It's true and *The 6 Indicators for Business & Life* is a game-changer for anyone interested in elevating themselves personally or professionally. He is a serious influence on those around him, with a wonderful sense of humor and playfulness that sets him apart from the rest. Now, you can get the benefit of his authentic outlook on life through the knowledge and thought-provoking content he shares in this new book."

Jamie Hartnett
Broadcast Executive/Brand Manager

INDICATOR

in·di·ca·tor
ˈindəˌkādər/
noun

1

1. a thing, especially a trend or fact, that indicates the state or level of something.

Imagine driving your car with no speedometer, the performance of your car wouldn't change although your reaction time to circumstances would be significantly affected. By the time you realized how fast you were going, it would be too late to make the necessary adjustments. In today's day and age, we have so many indicators to let us know virtually everything happening in our lives. We have heart rate monitors, step counters, apps to help us save money, calorie counters, and devices that tell how much actual sleep we enjoyed the previous night. We have information to evaluate all the information in our lives, yet most of us run with little to no awareness by which to gauge the real health of our business and life. What would it mean to you to have a way to evaluate, even measure the Character, and integrity that would be directly linked to the bottom line performance and more importantly the sustainability of your organization or relationship?

Driving 20 mph with no speedometer can be navigated relatively easy, but as you reach 80-100 mph, you need an Indicator in place that will increase your awareness and help you to prepare you to evaluate and act at a higher rate of velocity.

My Mom (mama as I call her) always told me to leave God room to surprise me, to never limit him. In telling me this, she always prepared me for where I was going as opposed to where we resided at the current moment. In all of her wisdom, my Mama seemed to always have a common theme, and that is to Prepare for greatness in all that you do! You have a plan and a purpose, and you will accomplish great things. So, build your life according to God's infinite plan!! She helped me to realize that with the right Indicators you can be better equipped to not only accept your current circumstances but to celebrate all that life brings!

FOREWORD

Kelly is a shining example of success achieved through the encouragement of others. His business practices personify and embody a simple principle: You don't build a business. You build People & then People build the business. As a result of a "servant-leadership" mentality, he has been able to advance his business and quality of life through the building and serving of others. What makes him a great leader is that he makes others feel that they can become great, and he pushes them to achieve greatness.

Kelly understands that people want to be recognized for their hard work and accomplishments and that they need to be acknowledged for their successes and achievements. Further, he understands that celebrating achievement is vital to the camaraderie of his team and the sustained success of his business. Kelly is respectful of others, and in turn, is respected himself. Not feared, simply because of his position, or liked because of his personality, but respected, meaning people recognize his expertise, knowledge, influence, trustworthiness and most importantly, his character and integrity.

I believe that if God has plans to greatly use you in the lives of others, you can expect your trials to be even greater than those of others. Kelly has always been willing to accept great responsibility and be accountable for not only his actions but the actions of his team. It's easy to take credit for the wins, bask in the glory of victory and reap the benefits of success. It's an entirely different thing to take responsibility for the loss, step forward in the face of defeat and be accountable, or acknowledge a mistake publicly or even privately. Kelly has always understood that people are watching and that his actions are being observed. As a result, he, more than anyone I've ever encountered, consistently demonstrates stability, integrity, and decisiveness - characteristics which help to make him an exceptional leader.

While compassionate, thoughtful and celebratory of others, Kelly has always been a producer of exceptional results - and people will always judge you on results. Whether measured in wins, hits, goals, pennies saved or dollars earned, production is always a measuring stick of success. Kelly recognizes this key component and expects and demands production and results from himself in much greater measures than he expects of others. I have never met a more motivated, driven, focused and determined individual in my life and I am blessed to have him as a business mentor, friend, and brother.

Kelly is the benchmark of great leadership, and although he has traveled the world, rubs elbows with the elite and captivates audiences on a global level, he has always remained grounded and humble in his approach. He knows where he is headed, but also, Kelly is remarkably cognizant of where he has come from.

Thirty years ago, Kelly and I lived in a one-bedroom apartment with our mom. We had no television, little food, and less money. We slept on the floor in sleeping bags and walked one mile to the bus stop each day to get to school… we had an abundance of love, lots of laughs and were admittedly somewhat naive about our ambitions. We had each other, which in our small world not only meant something, it represented everything.

They say ignorance is bliss, which in our case held true, because although we may have been aware of our circumstances, we were never defined by them and looked back, thankfully, we were simply unaware of the possibility of being limited by them. We managed to never speak about life regarding where we were, but where we were going, and today, although he has not yet arrived, I am so very proud of the direction Kelly is heading.

Thank you, Kelly, for demonstrating to me that there is no such thing as a dream that is too big… Only thoughts that are too small. Your example is awe-inspiring.

Robert Cardenas, Esq.
Cardenas Law Group

PREFACE

I remember sitting in a little hotel room in Tecumseh, Michigan when it hit me. Little did I know that my career up until this point was about to shift. We all have forks in the road when we are presented with a choice to continue down the same safe road or to embark on an adventure with an uncertain path where no footprints exist. My makeup as a person has always pushed for the "What if." And I have lived in the possibility that it might just work. I have always been a simple guy, sometimes a little too simple. I am what you would call an overly optimistic believer. I once said that if someone told me that Superman was outside, I would simply believe and if I went out and he wasn't there, I wouldn't call you a liar. I would say that he left. I never recommend this kind of thinking or mindset. I am only telling you so we can gain some context for our journey together.

I look at life through two different filters. The first one is a lens that most refer to as "Rose-Colored Glasses." I am pretty sure this comes from my upbringing. I was the baby in the family, and our family had a lot of chaos. My big brother Rob did everything in his power to protect me from any adversity. Now as I think about it, my Mom also embodied the same trait. She always had an amazing way of making us feel that we were the normal ones and that our circumstances were always a blessing! Thank you, Mama!

My second filter is a lens that breaks everything down to the lowest common denominator. This definitely came from my Pops, who you will hear a lot about through these pages. He is a dreamer and is one of the most determined people that I have ever met. Single focus comes to my mind when I think about him. He often referred to it as pit bull mentality. It's the thought process that consists of locking your jaws on to your desired focus and not letting go until it becomes your reality.

To him it was simple: If you want something, you focus on it, and by any means necessary you achieve the target. This type of thinking was passed down a generation, and that is what has created the simple being that I am. With my mom's optimism and love for life and my Pop's determination and simplistic focus, I feel that anything is possible as long as you are willing to work hard and stay in line with your purpose.

Tecumseh is a buzzing metropolis, and my hotel was that of the Four Seasons…that is how I remember it. It is a town of about 8,500. And my hotel was a cute and quaint place in the middle of this town. Ok, ok, if you haven't noticed, I live within my reality. And I would like to invite you in; the water is fine! In all my travels around the country and abroad, I have heard many concepts of business and relationships, but I had never experienced the fusion of the two in such a simple way. What was revealed to me that night blew me away, didn't allow me to sleep, and made me want to share it with the world!

My life has consisted of what my Pops refers to as the 98-2 rule—98% attitude and 2% aptitude. No, I don't see this as a negative or that my Pops didn't see me as intelligent. It meant to me that he believed in me and who I was more than just my education. As long as you continue to have a great attitude, life will present you with opportunities unimaginable. I have witnessed this first-hand in many areas of my life. A great attitude and the ability to truly be yourself will open so many doors.

I have never relied on how things were done in the past. Instead, I relied only on what I have been inspired to do, even when that seems like the impossible. My brother says that I have a golden horseshoe, and although I would love to believe that, I have simply been assured all of my life that it is a beautiful thing to be myself.

I cannot take credit for any of these concepts, as they were given to me free. Therefore, I want to give them freely to all who will listen. My life has been an example of this

98-2 theory, although it was unbeknownst to me until now. I guess this is like becoming the best parent that you can be, generally happens when you become a grandparent. So as I share this way of thinking, I want you to know that the real magic in all of it is YOU. It's only when you add your personality and purpose to these concepts, your true potential will be unlocked.

I truly believe that these six indicators can change the trajectory of the world as you know it. This may sound like a lofty goal but doesn't every concept that impacts on a grand scale? Let me ask you this: What would it mean to you to have a scorecard that you could base everything in your life from this point forward that would help to assess and create an action plan for your potential? Now, do I have your attention? In no way am I saying that I have all the answers. But in the chapters ahead, you will find the keys that will help you develop the right mindset as well as your Best Practices for success in all that you do.

It was about 11 p.m. when I had an epiphany. It was so clear to me. Success in business and relationships can be summed up in just 6 primary indicators. So, you can imagine just how excited I was. The next morning after about three hours of sleep, I shared it for the first time. I wish that I could tell you it changed the world we live in and I was propelled into the stratosphere. The exact opposite happened. That's right; I almost lost my audience. I spooked them!

I was so excited about this information and saw it so clearly, but it taught me a valuable lesson. Truth be told, my Pops had revealed that lesson to me years earlier, but as we all do, we must have practical application in our way of thinking to give credit to great ideas. As I write this, I realize just how silly that sounds. Are you like me, having had your parents tell you for years principles that you resisted only to "discover" them when you are around 25–30 years old and realize that they were right all along?

Enter my Lesson. My Pops told me years ago that he walked into a new company he was working for, sat down with the executives and told them he was going to cut costs by 50% and increase efficiency by 75%! You can imagine how they reacted... they were spooked! They wanted to tell him every reason why these things were not possible. Well, as you go through the journey of this book, I want you to know that I have heard about every excuse of how this couldn't be true and experienced an overwhelming amount of data that has encouraged me to know that it is that simple! After I shared these six indicators with my first audience, I didn't walk away discouraged. Conversely, their opposition to the concept inspired me to go out and explore business challenges for small and large companies to see if there was a place where these principles wouldn't apply. Throughout all of my research, I have concluded that every Question, Challenge, Catastrophe, Hurdle, Goal, or Mission can be

Answered, Solved, and Accomplished by applying these six indicators.

Oh, and by the way, here is an update on the first audience that was spooked and almost ran me off because of my wild projections. Megan, who is the director of the salon, has accomplished more than triple the goal that had originally almost sent her into cardiac arrest. And now in BHD Salon, the new normal has exceeded the outlandish goals that I set for them that day. This brings to mind any record that has been set is only the benchmark until someone chooses to focus on it, in which case, it becomes the norm. For example, consider the 4-minute mile. Until May 6, 1954, it was said that it was humanly impossible to accomplish such a feat. Roger Bannister, however, equipped with a pit bull mentality and a relentless work ethic would run a 3:59 mile on that day creating a new reality for all that came after him. The most amazing part of this is what came after. Within six weeks of Bannister's momentous run, Landy then broke that record finishing a mile in 3:57.9, and thirteen months after the four-minute mile becoming a reality, three more runners broke it in the same race. Do you see where I am going here? All it takes is for you to break through and then you can create a new normal for generations to come. Do you want to break through or do you simply want someone else to determine your ceiling?

Are you ready? Let's go!

Indicator #1

Culture

Although this is a buzzword nowadays, I would like to dig into it so that you know exactly what you are dealing with and where your focus is going to be.

cul·ture[1]

ˈkəlCHər/

noun

noun: **culture**

1.

the arts and other manifestations of human intellectual achievement regarded collectively.

- a refined understanding or appreciation of this. "men of culture"
- the customs, arts, social institutions, and achievements of a particular nation, people, or other social group.

the attitudes and behavior characteristic of a particular

---

1   https://en.oxforddictionaries.com/definition/culture

social group. "the emerging drug culture"

verb BIOLOGY

1.

maintain (tissue cells, bacteria, etc.) in conditions suitable for growth.

The main aspect of this that really jumped out at me was the clause—**maintain in conditions suitable for growth**.

As I read that, it moved me to my core and intensified my passion to have this as our first indicator. It seems as if the evidence keeps stacking up. There may be other aspects of the definition that hit you, or maybe you glossed over that part and wondered why I put it there. I believe we can learn a lot about our lives and existence through understanding the words that we use.

My Pops raised my brothers and me with the one phrase that we believe he knew how to speak in Spanish (he's actually fluent now but during the years we grew up, he had lost it and would only repeat this, with a really bad accent), "La Familia es todo, Porque si no es de la Familia no es de nada!" The loose translation is: "It's all about the family, and if it's not about the family, then it's not about anything." I know, you are going to correct me there, but this is my book; hence I get to write the rules. I heard this so many times throughout my childhood, and it was in my mid-20s that I started to understand the true meaning.

Some grow up with an amazing sense of their ancestry and the stories that made their family; others have an outline and fill in the blanks as they grow up, and still, others have no idea about where they came from. I used to associate these three scenarios with the amount of culture or lack of it. This couldn't have been further from the truth. In this chapter, we are going to break down culture not only from a literal standpoint but also from a practical application viewpoint. The first nugget of this chapter is about to be offered up!

[A nugget in this book is going to be a little piece of wisdom that has immense value if applied in the right area.]

Do you see what I just did there? This was the first of many points of practical application that we will use along this journey. Using the word Nugget could have so many meanings if left to interpretation, but I wanted to laser focus the direction. Boom, I am going to come at you like a spider monkey!

NUGGET:

**Every environment has a *culture*,
especially the ones that think they don't.**

Let me explain. I have a friend and mentor who was one of my first business partners. She is now one of the premier owners in the Paul Mitchell School network. She is also a salon owner, author, wife, and mother. Her name is Tina Black, and she is one of the most dynamic people that I have ever come across.

When she first opened her salon, she came to me for coaching. And after 3½ days of intense training, she made a statement to me on the ride to the airport that turned out to be one of the most valuable lessons I would ever learn. I was in the back seat of the car (I like to ride in the back seat when there are at least three people in the car because it makes me feel important) [insert emoji here] and she said, "Our Salon is just lacking culture, that is the challenge!"

It was like the dust cleared at that moment, and it was clear what the solution was. It was NOT the fact that they had "no culture." It was that their culture consisted of showing up late, dressing how they wanted, and having an independent mindset. All of this was in addition to many other challenges. I told her that according to that culture, her team was performing at 100%.

Every environment has a culture. Whether we are intentional about the principles of that culture is our choice. Let's look at the culture of In-N-Out Burger. The people of this company are committed to every one of their belief systems—even down to wearing a hat that is from the 1950s. When you step in closer and spend time with anyone who works inside the organization, they will tell you with conviction how amazing the company is. One of my best friends,

Dave, worked at In-N-Out in Las Vegas for about 4 years and through that time, I was able to experience a close-up look at how their culture operated. At first, I thought Dave was sold out to the concept simply because his pay dwarfed any other fast food position at the time. My thought process only lasted until I experienced the culture first hand. Dave invited me to a company get-together, a Wet-n-Wild, and I was shocked to see the camaraderie and love amongst the employees of a "fast food restaurant." What I witnessed that day, unbeknownst to me, would ultimately help shape the National Brand that I created years later.

Think of it: This is a company that sells burgers, fries, and shakes. The simplicity still blows my mind to this day. In-N-Out had the foresight to understand that they were going to be deliberate about their focus and were going to create a culture of people that were evangelists for their brand as opposed to selling a better burger at a lower price! I am getting goose bumps as I write this! This culture has lasted the test of time because of a ruthless adherence to their core principles. To this day, any In-N-Out location has a full line in the drive-thru from the time they open until closing time. I have never heard anyone complain that they don't have tacos or a breakfast menu. They choose not to chase trends. They continue to succeed because they chose the make-up of their culture as opposed to allowing it to develop on its own.

NUGGET:

Anything left unattended will choose
its own growth pattern.

Let us look at the opposite side of this coin. While we have looked at In-N-Out as an example of a deliberate culture and a highly predictable result, let's examine a culture that basically develops itself. My wife has a saying, "Stick to the Plan but go with the Flow." I believe that she adopted this mentality when we got together because she realized that our lives were not going to be anywhere close to normal. She has imparted so many amazing cultural aspects to our family without me ever realizing it until now. One specific example is that we read to our children every night for 20–30 minutes before they go to bed. You can imagine the long-lasting effects that my genius wife is counting on. That brings me to my point. Growing up for my brother and I was a bit different than this era. It was a different time and, our parents were working hard to make sure we had food on the table. They didn't have the technology and luxuries that we enjoy today! They worked long hours , sometimes multiple jobs and or shifts, so we were often left to take care of ourselves. No reading was done each night. And come to think of it, I only read **one full book** throughout my educational career. (*Island of the Blue Dolphins*, for those of you who were wondering which one.)

Most of my fondest memories in my life have to do with my big Brother Rob. This one, in particular, was when I was about 5–6 years old, and Rob was 7–8. We had a babysitter named Richard, and he wasn't, let's say, a cross-fit enthusiast. You feeling me? After a couple of weeks of Richard showing up and plopping down on our couch in front of the TV with a big bowl of OUR cereal, my brother (and protector) had had enough. The next night, my 8-year-old hero sat my Mom down and explained why Richard was not a fit and that he was going to relieve him of his duties and that she should back him in his decision. I am laughing as I write this. Can you imagine an 8-year-old having this conversation? My mom agreed, and from that point forward, Rob walked me home from school, took care of me and put me to bed at 9 o'clock, right after *Entertainment Tonight* (ET). My parents were separated at the time, and my Mom was going to school and working full time, so there was very little option. Being left on our own created a culture in our brotherhood that consisted of figuring things out, understanding how to make decisions, and realizing that there were consequences that followed. Do you see my "rose-colored glasses" in effect here? This could have been a recipe for disaster as you can imagine but because of the love and prayers of my Mom, everything turned out ok. Well, most things. Most scenarios like Rob's and mine don't turn out quite the same. When children are left unattended, just like any business they take on a life of their own. And most of the time, it is nowhere close to the initial intended result. My brother and I are the exceptions to the rule in this instance. And all of that praise goes to my Mom for her fervent and unrelenting prayers. She is in her own words our Family's **Prayer Warrior**.

NUGGET:

No matter the circumstance, prayer can override everything as long as you are willing to commit to it.

I know what some of you are thinking, *I can put this book down now and not worry about my culture anymore because I can just pray it through.* I wish it was that easy. The part that I didn't mention is the foundation that both of our parents imparted before the babysitter situation took place. So keep this book in your hands! I think you get the feel of what I mean now!

We are now going to break down *culture* into its lowest common denominator. At the base of any larger structure that lasts the test of time is a foundation. This is the aspect that receives the least credit. People are not going to compliment you on this until they see the results years after it is laid.

Years ago, when I bought my second home in Vegas, I was able to see this concept play out in my life. I was the third person to buy a home in the neighborhood, and I would visit the plot of land before there were even streets. I would drive through the dirt and escort my friends and family proudly to show them where my house would eventually be! I remember when they finally laid the foundation, I could see exactly, in my mind, the layout. My excitement far outweighed the excitement of the people that I shared this with. There was the lesson…

NUGGET:

The only person who will be excited about the foundation will be the one who is fully invested in the end result.

Let's lay the foundation!

Question #1 — What is Your Reason Why?

So many people come to me and ask about building their brand, and when I ask them this question, they go blank. Most try to recover by telling me the features of their product or service. Please stay on number one until it is crystal clear and rolls off your tongue. Better yet, it oozes from your pores! **Your reason why** is the single most important aspect of achieving success in all that you do!

My Pops always drove this home to my brothers and me as we were growing up. He would say: "Boy, people will always see your heart!"

You see, the heart is something you cannot fake. When we hire for our company, I look at people in their eyes and can generally tell if they are going to be a cultural fit. My reason **why** has always been pretty simple: **To leave things better than the way I found them!** When it applies to my industry, I am constantly looking to cut away the fat and streamline processes. In [2] my personal life I am searching for ways to elevate my family's life to give them a spring board that is far greater than the one I had as a child.

Financially, I want to learn the principles that will improve my way of life! Do you see the pattern here? Once you zero in on your reason **why**, it is easier to apply it to all aspects of your life! I even connected this to Carnival games...I told you, I live in my own world. Follow me here...

When I was a kid, my mom would give me and my brothers 3–5 dollars to go to the Flower Festival.[3] My brothers would spend their money carefully and responsibly on food, and then save the rest. But not me! I would head right for the games! And you know that with that amount of money, your chances were slim to none on winning a prize. This didn't deter me, and this was where my reason "why" was solidified. After losing all my money trying to win a stuffed animal, I would return to our one bedroom apartment and construct an exact (never taking all the details into account)

2   http://processes.in/
3   https://explorelompoc.com/event/lompoc-flower-festival/

replica of the game and practice for a year until the fair came back to town! After a couple of years without ever winning the heralded prize, I resolved to become so successful that I could have enough funds to play until I won!

This concept sounds so easy. But I have been shocked to encounter so many organizations and people that have skipped this foundational step. When we were growing up, my parents were completely supportive of anything we wanted to do, be it sports, art, music, or whatever under only one condition: that we did it to the best of our ability! Never in competition with anyone else, but giving 100% of our effort to that task! This was the reason why quitting was not allowed in our house. Everything has a reason **why** behind it and you can always tell the tree by its fruit. In a relationship, when a man presents his woman flowers only because he wants something in return or to cover something that he has done wrong that she doesn't know of, the flowers lose their meaning and the effect is nullified. On the other hand, when the reason **why** is communicated clearly, those same flowers can bring a spark of life back into the relationship.

Why did you start this business in the first place should be the question that is close to your cuff at all times. I was very fortunate to have my Pops reiterate to me constantly that the only reason he was in business was to be a service to people. This stuck with me, and although at times it caused me to make less in the short term, it allowed me to collect on the compounded interest of true relationships over the long haul. Some of you may be thinking, "I went into business for the only reason anyone should—to make MONEY." This reminds me of a friend named Chris whom I met on a plane years ago. What he said to me about nine years ago has stuck with me ever since. There are a couple of lessons in this one, so let me start from the beginning.

NUGGET:

Show up to the Airport early for your flight...always!

I arrived at the airport about 52 minutes before my flight (maybe less but that is how I remember it). In my mind, I was thinking that all I needed to do was check in 45 minutes before my flight because that was the cut off to check bags. So I reasoned the 7 minutes that I had to get through the line should be ample enough. However, as I entered the terminal, I realized that there was going to be a challenge. But with my optimism anything was possible, right? Wrong. The line was so long and slow moving that by the time I was next up to the ticket counter, my flight was due to leave in 20 minutes. My normally cheerful mood was traded in for a tense and focused demeanor.

The ticket agent smiled politely and asked how she could help me. I told her that I was on a scheduled flight to Michigan and she did the normal head down, type fast, shaking head as she looked at the computer screen while making unidentifiable sounds with her mouth that translated to me there was no way I was getting on the plane. She then let me know that there was nothing else available to that destination, only to machine gun type again and say, "Hold on. You have only one option. There is one seat available on a flight that will get you there at the same time." Before she could even finish saying this, I said, "Yes! I will take it." She looked at me sheepishly and said, "Sir, it is in First Class, and you will have to pay the full price of $1100 to secure the seat."

My jaw dropped, and I called my Pops to get some advice. I assumed that he was going to justify my desire to scrap the trip because of the circumstance, although from even with the limited information that you have of my Father, you know that wasn't going to happen. When I got him on the phone and told him my side of the story, he quickly dropped knowledge on me like he always does. He asked me one question and then hit me with his simple theory: "Son, did you commit to being there?" My answer was obviously yes. At that point, he cleared the fog of doubt and told me that it was the cost of doing business, that I needed to honor my commitments, and that I should get excited because God was going to bring a blessing if I started to praise Him immediately for my circumstances. He then reminded me that I was the Greatest, that he believed in me, and that this story would be worth far more than the $1100 I was about to invest.

Even after the pep talk, my attitude was poor at best, and as I stormed through the airport with my *Beats by Dre* headphones, I tried not to make eye contact with anyone. I arrived at my gate after going through expedited security clearance of my First Class ticket. Even that experience didn't lift my spirits.

NUGGET:

Sometimes our attitude can make even the most magic of moments seem like a chore!

When I finally boarded the plane, I took my seat in First Class. I had dreamed of moments like this when I was a kid, and now here I was with a salty attitude while boarding First Class and being waited on hand and foot. I dropped down in my seat and stared straight ahead, turned up my music and anxiously awaited the plane to take off. My pouting was abruptly interrupted by the man sitting next to me grabbing one of my earphones and asking how I was doing. I was shocked by this gesture, and I had no idea the blessing that it was going to be. He introduced himself as Chris and would not allow me to continue in my dark mood. He asked me positive questions, replied with a bright side appeal, and kept me thinking for the entire flight from Las Vegas to Minneapolis. About halfway through the conversation, he told me of a man who worked for him who had come into his office and demanded a raise. The man explained that all he needed was $150,000 and his problems would be solved. Chris didn't hesitate. He pulled out a check and filled it out for $150,000 and signed it to the man. As Chris handed the check over and the man grabbed hold of it, Chris reinforced his grip, looked him in his eyes and asked, "Now, what are you going to do with this money?" The man's response was, "I am going to pay off my mom's house and buy a boat." Chris snatched the check back from him and told him to simply focus on that and not the money, and he would surpass his need. BOOM! People think that money will save them and in reality, there is always a reason **why** behind that desire. When you focus on the **Why,** the **what** will inevitably be yours.

When you are embarking on a culture whether it be in business or personal, your reason **why** must be the foundation of all that you do. It will bring you back to center, keep you on track and aid you in your darkest times. Keep it simple and always know WHY you are doing what you are doing!

NUGGET:

Your reason "why" doesn't have to be complicated or righteous. It only needs to be the signature to who you are!

Question #2 — What is Your Story?

I love stories. I have made an amazing life for my family by being a storyteller! You must know your story and tell it often.

NUGGET:

The more you tell your story, the deeper your desire will be for it to be interesting!

Think of your life as a movie. Does it make sense? Would you watch it? Are you the leading actor? These are questions by which I constantly evaluate my life! Through my travels, I find that when I tell my story, people want to be a part of it. They invest in the outcome. It creates a force that almost takes on a life of itself that far exceeds expectations. Your life's work is the constructing of your story. Everyone has one, and it's up to you to make sure that it is engaging. The more interesting your story is, the easier it is to accomplish your goals. I just learned in Michael Eisner's book *Work-*

ing Together: Why Great Partnerships Succeed[4] that the sum
of 1+1 equals more than 2. He chronicles the partnerships
of some of the great companies in their respective industries,
and all of them have this common thread. When we create
partnerships, we call on the strengths of others to help with
our deficiencies. I am not advocating that everyone go out
and get a partner. I am, however, saying that if you have
people engaged in your story and they become evangelists of
your "movie," then it can have a snowball effect.

Every person in your organization should be invested
in your story. Once this takes place, the people who con-
sume your culture will follow suit. Stories build, destroy and
maintain culture all in how they are told. This is why you
must be a great storyteller through your words, actions, procedures, successes, and failures.

Guests Who Fly 2,500 Miles to Get Their Hair Done

Lori and Jay Thompson have been my guests for over 14
years. They fly into Vegas from West Palm Beach to get their
hair done. You read that right, stay with me! When we first
met, I was working for a company, and they became engaged
with my story. I told them about my journey in the industry
and how I was working in my dream job that I had chased
for over 2½ years. Over the course of our relationship, I was
fired from my job, rented a chair, opened my first salon,

4   https://www.amazon.com/Working-Together-Great-Partnerships-Succeed/
    dp/0061732443/ref=tmm_pap_swatch_0?_encoding=UTF8&qid=&sr=

27

opened six more, shut down two, became a school owner, traveled all over the world speaking and teaching the fusion of art and business, got married, had kids, and moved to California amongst a couple other things. Lori and Jay are not just my guests in the salon—they play major roles in my movie! They continue to invest in my story because they have ownership of it.

Kathy and Marie Veverka are not only guests of mine in the salon they are friends that i have had over the last 18 years. The fly into Vegas from Scottsdale and generally only stay a couple of hours and fly right home. Originally, I met Kathy because one of her neighbors in Arizona used to visit her daughter in Vegas and recommended my services.

NUGGET

**Creating Evangelists will help
to grow your influence exponentially.**

On our first visit i would have to say that i didn't deliver the greatest product to Kathy. She was actually pretty upset with me about her haircut. That is until she sat down on her return flight home and was hit on by the guy next to her, and guess what? He started off the conversation by complimenting her hair!! Thank you Baby Jesus! Since that visit we have seen each other for the last 18 years on a 6-8 rotation. Kathy then brought her daughter Marie and i tell you that the apple doesn't fall far from the tree. The heart and souls of these 2 individuals have helped me to realize that you don't have to rush anything. Great things will come to the great at heart!!!! Kathy never spoke much about herself , so one day i decided to ask. She simply said, I am an artist and left it at that. Come to find out she is one of the most revered artists of our time. Two former Presidents have her pieces hanging in their home. So you can imagine my reaction when she told me that she had created a whole collection from my image. Marie just came off the set of "The Avengers" new movie working on the production side and is working on her first screenplay. Throughout our relationship Kathy and Marie have always believed in me and the vision of where I was going. They both are constantly spreading the word where ever they go because they have helped to create the foundation, they are invested.

My relationship with Kathy and Marie is so very import-ant to me and transcends a salon visit. One of my favorite stories of Kathy was in the early 2000's. She was in the hos-pital in Washington State and was not feeling so well. The doctor gave strict orders for her to stay in bed(in the hos-pital) until further notice. Well, When you meet Kathy you will understand this but for now just follow me, She wait-ed until the doctor left the room. She took out her IV got dressed , got a cab to the airport, flew to Las Vegas so i could do her hair and returned to the hospital before the doctor knew she was gone. As she told me the story that day, I was honored but wanted to know why coming to the salon was so important. My ego told me it was because of my superior skills, but Kathy brought my career and life into perspective by telling me that she need to "FEEL" beautiful. This had nothing to do with her physical appearance, it had all to do with putting a smile on her face she told me. She is an Angel in my life and I am so blessed to know her, although she is never wants any credit and she is constantly pumping me up!!! I have the best Job in the world!!!!!

Diane and Jeff Koznick have been a God send from the time that we met. I was working in Las Vegas at the Mandalay Bay and was posed with the opportunity to work in San Diego for about 10 days. While I was there I encountered a young gentleman that would get his hair colored dark brown every 2 weeks. The reason why this was so intriguing is that he had naturally red hair making this something that I wanted to understand. I engaged in conversation with him and never really thought much more about it. Fast forward a couple of months and I am back in Las Vegas. I have a new guest that comes in and our connection was instantaneous. She was magnetic and lit up the room! She complimented everyone and seemed to give people the permission to believe in their greatness! As we talked I asked her how she had heard about our salon. She informed me that her step-son Charlie had a friend that went to our salon in San Diego

(The red head that frequented the salon) and that he recommended me when she inquired where to get her hair taken care of.

NUGGET

You never know who you are dealing with, where they have been or where you will meet up with them again. So make a friend out of everyone!, my Pops would always say!!!!

Little did I know that DIANNE would become one of the most influential people in my life. Her husband Jeff or "KOZIE" as DIANNE calls him, has also been a source of inspiration in my life. DIANNE was and is one of the most powerful executives in the fashion industry, although she only ever wanted to put the focus on my accomplishments. To put in perspective who she is, one time I had a pair of jeans that I asked if she could have them repaired because she worked with the company that produced them. After a couple of weeks she returned to the salon to let me know that she was sorry that they couldn't fix them . She then let me know that the head designer felt so bad that he wanted to make a pair of jeans custom for me with my logo on them. The brand was Levi's!!!!!

DIANNE and "Kozie" helped me to expand my vision of life and realize that there was a world out there that was unbeknownst to me. Through the years we have shared many stories, accomplishments, and memories. Through it all they have believed in my potential not just my reality. They are invested in a story that they have helped to create.

Charlene Foss was getting a pedicure at the salon that I was directing. She had just come off a cruise and had experienced a not so favorable haircut. I was introduced to her and as I looked at it, I assured her that with a couple of minor adjustments, I could make her happy again. That was the beginning of a beautiful friendship. We have been so much together. I had the pleasure of watching her daughter grow up, graduate high school, college, and now flourish in her career as a professional. Charlene has traveled from her home in Hilton Head, South Carolina to Las Vegas, Carlsbad, and Chicago. Charlene has believed in me since I was a baby in my industry and has referred many of her friends and family to the salon. But more importantly, she tells the story to all of the people that question why she would fly across the country to see a hairdresser.

David and Julia Hamilton have played such a huge part in the success not only of me personally but of our brand as a whole. I met Julia in 1999 when she worked with my brother. He gave her my services as a gift for Christmas. Once we connected, she brought in her husband David, one of the premiere genius minds in the medical billing industry. He is a true pioneer and has helped elevate my mind-frame.

I then met Brittany, their beautiful and talented daughter. I believe Brittany was 3 or 4 years old when I first met her and my wife and I just did the hair for her wedding. She is now an authority in the Eyelash industry and owns her own business, SoCal Beauty, which she opened before she was 19 years old. My relationship with the Hamilton's started in Las Vegas and has continued through Chicago, San Diego, Carlsbad, and Salt Lake City. They are invested in our story and have ownership of everything that we do.

Julie and Eric Compton are the reason why I even have the opportunity to write this book. They are amplifiers of all things good. They both see potential in people and are willing to invest time , money and most importantly their hearts in making sure that people have a better life!

I met Julie at a seminar I was doing and she hired me into her salon to work with her crew. In all of my years of traveling I have never been spoiled the way Julie did when i would come and do work for her. I resisted it at first and then i realized that it wasn't material thing it was her truly giving from her heart. Our friendship was really solidified when, in 2006, I lost my job. She called me every morning and gave me encouraging words and imparted the wisdom that I needed to get out there and keep working hard! The morning after i was fired i will never forget the phone call she gave me! I can hear her voice now, her words would stick with me and be the foundation for a multi-million dollar company just 7 years later. Are you ready for it???? I think it should be a nugget, You?

NUGGET

"You have 24 hours to feel mad, sad , angry or whatever emotion you want, after that you are going to get your A@# up and go GET A JOB!!!!"

Through Julie I met the kindest human I have ever experienced, Eric! Eric is one of the top Dentists in the world in addition to being an entrepreneur, angel investor, husband, father, and amazing friend. He has taught me to be the absolute best at your craft through studying the game. He is constantly educating himself and has an innate ability to help you expand your capacity. Many people at his level are good in areas and extremely deficient in others. For instance a lot of people are successful in their business and the family suffers. This is not the case with Eric, he is the anomaly, he is equally great at all aspects of life. Our friendship has enabled many wonderful memories, but one sticks out to me most. Peyton Manning was returning to Indianapolis for the first time after signing with Denver. I called Eric and asked if he wanted to go. He responded with the answer any football fan would, and we sat on the 40 yard line about 12 rows up. The game was cool but the real magic was to see Eric one of the most successful and powerful guys I know not have a care in the world and be a kid again, even if it was for a couple of hours!

Julie and Eric have invested in me in all aspects of my life. We are partners in our Chicago salon as well as a Paul Mitchell School in Green Bay. My life has changed because of these 2 individuals not because I was looking for someone to do business with but because I shared my story with them, they became engaged and desired to be a part it.

I could make a whole book out of the guests that I have had the pleasure of taking care of, but I would like to tell you the story of one more. Michelle Tamangawa is one of the first guests that I ever had in the professional beauty industry. We started working together in Memphis, Tennessee, and our relationship has taken us through Salt Lake, San Diego, and Las Vegas. Now, she lives in Brooklyn, New York, and commutes to Chicago to tend to her *locks*. She will generally fly into Chicago at 9 a.m. I will do her hair, and she will be back on a plane en route to NYC by about 2:30 p.m. Now that is commitment. Michelle and I have gone through life together on a six-week schedule. She has invested so much in me over the years that I would not be here without her belief. She is not only a part of my story, she is my story. We often laugh about the changes in our lives. She was in college when we first met, and I was less than one year into my career. Oh, how times have changed!

First and foremost, people want to identify with the story of your culture. And when they do that, they take owner-ship of it. This is where you can multiply without spending money to manufacture connections. This is true in relation-ships also. My wife and I have a really cool Love Story and although not perfect, the people around us are invested in it and constantly encourage it to get better.

Early on with our company, I chose deliberately not to bring on a PR agency because I wanted to develop roots and authenticity to our story before we exposed it on a grand scale. Yes, it is a longer and slower process but it is amazing now that we work with **One7**, the Top PR firm in Las Ve-gas. Since our story is true and has substance, it is so natural to tell it. We don't have to reach for stories to tell. They are constantly being constructed every day within our culture. Be very careful that your story is true and authentic before you start to tell it because—

NUGGET:

**Everything that is produced in the dark
will come to light at some point.**

Your culture hinges on your ability to tell your story!

Question #3 — What is Your Definition of Success?

Through my travels around the world, I rarely get the same answer to this question. It's all relative to your perspective. I told you that my vision of success is having enough money to win stuffed animals at the carnival. Yours may be a specific salary in mind, a certain number of days that you want to work, or you want to simply pay your rent on time. Your definition isn't as important as the fact that you zero in on it. Once you know your definition of success, you can set benchmarks and write an action plan to ensure you attain your potential! I was at a hair show in Traverse City and asked this question. A lady raised her hand and said, "Working 7 days a week!" I replied immediately that I didn't want to be successful according to her standards! A healthy *culture* has a clear definition of success that can be adapted in principle by all of those on your team.

A laser focused view of success doesn't mean that everyone has to value the same thing. For example, in our culture, Sara Bryan,[5] our Vice President loves the finer things in life. She loves shoes and not just the ones that cover her feet. She loves the ones with red bottoms as well!

Jenn Moses,[6] one of the most efficient hairdressers in our company, views performance as nothing more than a score…and she loves to win! It's no wonder that she has been

---

5   https://www.kellycardenassalon.com/team/sara-bryan
6   https://www.kellycardenassalon.com/team/jenn-moses

the top performer for the last six years straight.

Christina Delaney[7] loves progress and is motivated by seeing her team grow, Ashlee Smith[8] loves to hear *thank you*. All of these different definitions of success are in line with the core of our culture. So you see, you can have individual desires and goals inside one common culture. Something that I was deliberate with early on was to identify what I thought a high-level hairdresser was. I obviously learned from the mentors I had who helped me to shape my views. An example of this is that I wanted a hairdresser to have a 4-day work week. I said it over and over to the first couple of team members and instilled in them that one day that would be the norm. Through repetition of that definition of success, we now have kids in our assistant program that have their sight set on that already.

My reason **why** on the 4-day work week was the superior quality of life the hairdressers could enjoy. You see, if you live a great life, you can give great service, which increases demand, in turn raising your rate, that ultimately increases the value you deliver to the guest. Also, it enables you to do less, be paid more, and enjoy your life! Do you understand the cycle? You see how I did that. I connected my reason **why** by telling a story of the definition of success. You will find that this is all intertwined and that success in relationship or business must have all the components. Otherwise,

7   https://www.kellycardenassalon.com/team/christina-delaney
8   https://www.kellycardenassalon.com/team/ashlee-smith

the relationship or business will not function at its capacity.

Now is the time to sit down and write out your definition of success.

Remember, every environment has a *culture* and you can either choose the values within, or they will develop on their own. I highly recommend that you choose your values wisely.

What is the threshold for your belief system?

This is a loaded question and one that is commonly answered quickly based on intentions as opposed to facts and data. I am a huge UFC fan and have been so since the inception of the sport. Years ago, there was a guy named James "Lights Out" Toney.[9] He was a champion boxer who would routinely put opponents to sleep (knock them out for you non-boxing fans). Toney thought it would be a good idea to challenge Randy Couture[10] who was the UFC champion at the time. Toney said that he was going to fight Couture at his discipline and show the world that boxing was the superior sport. The challenge was that Couture had been training in Mixed Martial arts for over a decade and Toney would have 3–4 months to train in this new style of fighting.

The hype leading up to the fight was amazing, and the trash talk was second to none. The night of the fight when the bell rang for the first round, everyone held their breath.

9   https://en.wikipedia.org/wiki/James_Toney
10   https://en.wikipedia.org/wiki/Randy_Couture

Toney charged Couture and swung with all his power! Couture ducked the hay-maker and took Toney to the mat with ease. And once he was on the mat, Toney had no idea what to do. It wasn't in his muscle memory with the limited training that he had. After a few punches to the head, Toney had all but given up. Couture put him in a choke hold and ended his night! All said and done, the fight lasted just over 90 seconds.[11]

You see, *Theory is good until you get punched in the face.* Once that happens, all bets are off, and we resort back to our muscle memory[12] or our core. When you are developing your Culture or better yet, when you are conceptualizing it, you must ask yourself these **4** questions before you are even close to the adversity that is inevitable in all cultures.

1. **What is your reason WHY?**
2. **What is your story?**
3. **What is your definition of success?**
4. **What is your threshold for your belief system?**

My wife,[13] then my girlfriend, asked me this question when I was going to open my first business. We were driving

---

11 http://www.telegraph.co.uk/sport/othersports/boxing/7970297/James-Toneys-lights-put-out-by-MMA-legend-Randy-Couture-on-UFC-debut-in-Boston.html
12 http://lifehacker.com/5799234/how-muscle-memory-works-and-how-it-affects-your-success
13 http://92011magazine.com/2012/10/07/family-comes-first-for-the-owners-of-the-kelly-cardenas-hair-salon-in-carlsbad/

to see the construction that was going on and she asked, "What happens if this doesn't work out?" I simply replied, "I will work harder!" This was right in line with the Culture that I wanted to create, that can be summed up in three words—***Commitment Eliminates Option***.[14]Whatever you are committed to eliminates the option of anything contrary to that commitment. I inquire about the threshold of culture all the time and most of the time, the answer is different than the reaction in troubled times. When you set out to shape a culture, you must sell out to it before it even begins.

Here is a great example. About five years ago, I had a girl who didn't want to work with us anymore, but she didn't know how to quit. I decided I wanted to make it better for her. So I asked her the question, "Do you want to stay?" She couldn't answer, and I knew that was her answer. The only challenge was that she was very talented and she had a circle of friends that would leave with her if she did.

Rewind to when I started the company. I had made the decision that I wanted a culture where people wanted to be there and no matter who they were or what they produced, if they didn't want to be there, then they needed to go. Coming back to the present, I knew that if she left and took her friends, I would lose over a half a million dollars in revenue that year. My decision had already been made five years pri-

---

14   http://www.paulmitchellpro.com/wordpress/2015/07/commitment-eliminates-options/

or, and my threshold for my culture was tested. Everyone in any type of relationship—be it business or personal—is going to be challenged on their ability to stick to their core values and I believe that if we are conscious, deliberate, and honest about where we stand, decisions down the line will be simple…although not easy.

When you are looking at your business or relationships, the first thing to evaluate is your culture. Your reason **Why** will help people to **buy in** to your story. A clear definition of success will help to strengthen the threshold of your belief system and make it a sustainable culture.

Based on the points in this chapter, please stop now and evaluate your culture. I would like you to score it from 1–10. Remember to be honest and score based on data and not intention. Ask yourself, "What is my reason **Why**? What is my story? Is it authentic? What is my definition of success?" And finally, "What is my threshold for my belief system?" You have now started the journey, and the great thing about life is that if you score lower than you like, you can always Make It Better!

Score yourself on a scale of 1–10 based on your awareness and creation of a healthy culture:

Circle One:

1   2   3   4   5   6   7   8   9   10

INDICATOR #1 NUGGETS

Every environment has a *culture*, especially
the ones that think they don't.

Anything left unattended will choose
its own growth pattern.

No matter the circumstance, prayer can override
everything as long as you are willing to commit to it.

The only person who will be excited about
the foundation will be the one who is fully
invested in the end result.

Show up to the Airport early for your flight…always!

Sometimes our attitude can make even the most
magic of moments seem like a chore!

Your reason "why" doesn't have to be complicated
or righteous. It only needs to be the signature
to who you are!

The more you tell your story, the deeper your
desire will be for it to be interesting!

Creating Evangelists will help to grow
your influence exponentially.

You never know who you are dealing with, where they
have been or where you will meet up with them again.
So make a friend out of everyone!, my Pops would
always say!!!!

"You have 24 hours to feel mad, sad , angry or whatever
emotion you want, after that you are going to get your
A@# up and go GET A JOB!!!!"

Everything that is produced in the dark
will come to light at some point.

INDICATOR #2

VIBE

vibe |vīb|[15]
noun *informal*
1 (usually **vibes**) a person's emotional state or the atmosphere of a place as communicated to and felt by others: *a lot of moody people giving off **bad vibes**.* [abbreviation of *vibrations*.]

I love this word so much! It jumps off the page at me and makes me think of going to my favorite club of all time. It was called the G Lounge. That name is even Gangster. I am a huge fan of Hip Hop and this place boasted of the best DJs for that genre of music. I could count on a non-mainstream playlist that would keep my head knocking and my feet moving all night long. Although it wasn't just the music, it was the decor, the way people were dressed and the lingo that was used in addition to all of the other details that made this place so incredible. I can still picture it now, and it has been over 20 years since I stepped foot in what I consider to

15   http://www.encyclopedia.com/humanities/dictionaries-thesauruses-pictures-and-press-releases/vibe-0

be my standard that all clubs are held to. Are you feeling me?

One of my favorite places to research is the Four Seasons Resorts. My researching consists of staying in their properties, and experiencing their amenities and relaxing. Some would see this as merely a vacation, but I see it as official business. The first time that I arrived at the **happiest** place on earth—no not Disneyland, I am speaking of the Four Seasons Resort in Maui[16]— I immediately caught the Vibe! There was an aura that let me know I had nothing to worry about, everything was taken care of, and I was going to be treated like a king with a sincere personal touch that was adapted to my personality. From the very first moment, I could feel that the people were engaged in the culture and they truly believed that this was their normal. In some arenas, you can sense that the people are trying to exceed their capacity of service because that is what they are told to do. This, however, is different. It is the greatest service far exceeding all the others in their industry, and it is natural to them because everyone has a great understanding of their reason **why** and how important it is to their own livelihood. I think that if you want to be successful in your business or relationships, you need to become a **research** connoisseur of all the leaders in their chosen industries. Each will have its own unique vibe, and you will have the opportunity to glean greatness from everyone.

---

16   https://www.fourseasons.com/maui/

I actually love to study small hole- in -the wall places too. Local businesses are some of my favorites to expand my understanding of vibe! Probably the best example of this is my favorite restaurant Fish 101,[17] located in Leucadia, CA. This place is an absolute phenomenon. Culture, Vibe, and the best food hands down! Fish 101 actually embodies every one of the six indicators and scores high in each one. Although no one is perfect, these guys are on point! Not only is their food superior, their team is engaged, their service is flawless, and most of their customers are evangelists. I would venture to say that a FISH 101 *hat* is the most popular hat in all of North County San Diego! They have created a culture and zeroed in on a vibe that has taken on a life of its own. Never be mistaken. I can assure you that environments like this no matter how laid back or relaxed they seem, are products of carefully constructed systematized plans. To create magic is one thing but to sustain it takes focus and adherence to your core principles. As I write this, I can almost feel the energy. Much like our first indicator and the next four that you will encounter, *vibes* exist whether you choose them or not. My advice is to be deliberate so that your vibe will be exactly how you desire it. My intention in this chapter is to give you the framework to construct any type of vibe that you want. The questions that lie ahead are meant to spark inspiration that will help this indicator to take on a life of its own.

17   http://fish101restaurant.com/

Happy isn't always the answer!

This may sound strange especially to the current generation. Many companies have built their vibe around **Happy** only to find that production starts to slip. Conversely, some build their *vibe* on the bottom line and realize that people aren't just numbers. I believe that once you identify and start to establish your culture, your vibe can evolve monthly, weekly, even daily as long as it is in line with your culture. A wise man once told me, "People respect what you inspect." So I have come to the conclusion that if you want something to grow or get better, you simply have to pay attention to it.

Take a second right now and grade your vibe on a scale of 1–10. Write it down on a piece of paper and put it away for now. We will come back to it. I learned that *happy isn't always the answer* in one of our businesses. Actually, I have learned that too much of one vibe isn't good for any environment. Would you like to hear an example? I already have your attention, but I wanted you to feel as if you are a part of the decision making. I had a leader in my company who was amazing at creating happiness. In fact, I have never experienced anything like it. It was as if she could sprinkle her magic on all of those around her. Not everyone wants the same thing right? We established that in the last chapter when we defined success.

NUGGET:

Anytime you try to create only one exclusive VIBE, you run the risk of alienating a larger percentage of your crew!

Your vibe is something that should be ever changing and based on the ways your culture needs to improve.

NUGGET:

If you want to improve an area of your environment, simply change the vibe!

Two Nuggets so fast…should we take a second to let them sink in…Nah…We are on a roll!

How do You Want to be Viewed Internally and Externally?

One of the most important areas in business to me when I started was that guests and my team looked to me the same. I had been around so many organizations in my life that treated their customers like gold and secretly, the employees didn't like each other. Actually, this is how it is in most companies. I would witness great customer service until I got behind the curtain and I could see that people would adhere to the systems but never really believe in the reason **why** behind it. Now, this isn't an indictment. We have all been there, right? Maybe it's a relationship that we know isn't the one and we go through the motions anyway. There are countless examples like this in all of our lives, so I am not acting like I am immune to this. Alright, since we are on the same page now, let's get to the business of making this better.

NUGGET:

True customer service is nothing more than a bi-product of authentic relationships between the team members of the organization or company.

As with any of these questions that we explore, we must dig deeper to create the environment that we truly desire. So, let's start with **How** you want to be viewed internally. Your foundation starts with how your crew views the environment. You must develop systems with a strong reason **why** in place. This will create buy-in from your team. I can remember early on in my career working at a salon in Memphis. It was my first taste of the professional industry. No one really spoke about the vision of the company and its leaders. Sure, if someone asked, we could recite some narrative that was our own interpretation of what we had heard or experienced. This left too much open space for the team to dictate the vibe of our culture.

NUGGET:

You must be specific and deliberate with your intentions to get the desired result in anything that you do.

Boom! Now that you understand this, let's set some specific goals for how you want to be viewed internally. I always wanted people to "want to" be at work, not "have to." I also wanted people to speak about me in a positive light, not just when I was there. If you are a leader and you think that you are in the clear because of what you hear your staff saying about you, please dig deeper and make sure it is the same as what you are *not* hearing. As a leader, this will take focus and most of all, an action plan. You don't have to walk on eggshells, but you must understand that if you want your crew to view you in a certain way, you must have your actions in line with that vision. Let's take, for example, that you want people to be efficient and on time. They must witness small acts of this in your character. So many managers (not leaders) feel that they have to put on an act when they are at work which causes a lot of internal confusion and ultimately, stress and resentment toward their work environment. Think about it in a relationship when you are with someone that you cannot be your true self when they are around. It takes twice as much effort and is doomed to end at some point. As a leader, if you believe in the *vibe* that you are trying to accomplish, then you can naturally create it. It will be

51

effortless because you are connected to it and see the value. If you find yourself exhausted from leading people because you feel that you have to "turn yourself on" when you are around them, I invite you to search your heart. This is a symptom of not believing wholeheartedly in the mission at hand. When you believe in the goal, it becomes a part of you and I guarantee that you will never become tired of being yourself!

I wanted people to see the value of their environment and to be evangelists for their mission. I believe this has to be intentional. Hence, when people come to me with challenges about how their company is viewed internally, I instantly check to see if they were deliberate about how they targeted the vibe. There are always exceptions to the rule, but in the majority of cases when you set your target before you shoot, you have a higher probability of accomplishing your goal. You may want to be viewed as disciplined, fun-loving, or efficient; there is not a right answer to this question. Once you decide the target, it is time to put systems in place to help your desire become a reality.

We wanted our company to all be on the same page, and the only way was through communication. This seemed so silly to the original five people that started our company because they thought since we work together all week, we already know each other. So when I scheduled a meeting every week for an hour, I received so much push back. The comments ranged from *what is the point of this* all the way to *this is a waste of time.* I knew however that if we were going to grow and accomplish our ultimate goal, we were going to have our systems and foundation in place. When we opened our Chicago location, logistics became a challenge. But with every challenge, there is joy in the solution and the process of finding it! (Rose-Colored glasses) This was a deliberate way for me to create the internal view in our company.

NUGGET:

Uninhibited constant communication will break down all walls.

My Pops always asks me what people fail at the most and work on the least? Communication! Thanks, Pops! I wanted an environment where there was open communication. That is one of the ways I wanted our company to be viewed internally because I believed that it would set us up for our future.

Now for the external. This is from the viewpoint of the client or consumer of your product or service. The internal will always help shape the external, and they will always be connected. If you go back to the last nugget, you will see that customer service is a bi-product of authentic relationship. That being said, the external or consumer view will actually be shaped by the internal view…MIND-BLOWN? It simply means the precise way you want your consumer to view you should be the main focus of how you want your crew to view the company. On the flip-side of this, if your internal view is at odds with the external or vice-versa, you will create a lot more work for yourself. Now, these principles are only applicable if you want a high level, healthy environment that will last the test of time. However, if you are not looking for a high level, healthy environment, just skip this part.

How Can You Manipulate the VIBE in Your Environment?

A couple of years ago, my kids fell in love with the movie *Despicable Me*. One of the songs on the soundtrack was "Happy" by Pharell Williams.[18] I was blown away by this song. So on the following Tuesday when we had our meeting, I arrived early and asked to have the song playing as people walked in. This changed the Vibe. It made people **happy**…Go figure! I made this a ritual and learned a lesson in the process.

NUGGET:

Too much of one thing can kill the desire for it.

---

18   https://en.wikipedia.org/wiki/Happy_(Pharrell_Williams_song)

I know what you are thinking right now, and it is quite ironic, right? Too much *Happy* made people mad, resentful, and a couple more emotions that weren't intended. People actually got sick of hearing "Happy." There was my lesson. This vibe manipulator need not be thrown away, only adjusted to make it great. I created a system that allowed a new person to choose the song we opened to every day. Simple, right? Yes, and so effective. The person who chooses the song on a specific day is attuned to hear their favorite tune, and their joy radiates to all of those around them. This was a deliberate act to **manipulate** the vibe. It doesn't have to be just about music. Maybe you allow one team member to choose the type of food that week for lunch. There are so many creative ways that you can manipulate the Vibe in your environment.

The other day, both my kids wanted to just watch their devices, and I wanted them to play outside. So after trying the "GET OUTSIDE and have fun whether you like it or not" method, I took a piece of paper and wrote down 7 words on it and challenged my kids to a Scavenger Hunt.[19] They went crazy, ran around the neighborhood and not only completed the whole list but also asked for another list.

---

19   https://en.wikipedia.org/wiki/Scavenger_hunt

NUGGET:

A manager will react to the vibe of their environment, but a leader will create systems that will deliver their desired Vibe.

I think that we have to go back to a childlike (not child-ish) mindset and have some fun with this. I have been using the word *manipulate*, so let's look at the real definition.

manipulate |məˈnipyəˌlāt|[20]
verb *[with object]*
1 handle or control (a tool, mechanism, etc.), typically in a skillful manner: *he manipulated the dials of the set.*
• alter, edit, or move (text or data) on a computer.
• examine or treat (a part of the body) by feeling or moving it with the hand: *a system of healing based on manipulating the ligaments of the spine.*
2 control or influence (a person or situation) cleverly, unfairly, or unscrupulously: *the masses were deceived and manipulated by a tiny group.*
alter (data) or present (statistics) so as to mislead.

You see, this is not a negative—to handle or control typically in a skillful manner—and you realize that you can use

20   http://www.encyclopedia.com/humanities/dictionaries-thesauruses-pictures-and-press-releases/manipulate-0

these vibe manipulators to create anything you want. One of our team members came up with the idea of a prayer board in all of the dressing rooms and bathrooms in our salons. This was an unintentional vibe manipulator that has created unimaginable magic. It's simply a piece of Plexiglas with a frame around it with the words "Prayer Requests," but the meaning behind it has given it new life. In every tour of the salon where we explain the environment to all first-time guests, we explain that they could write their prayer request on the board and that they would have all 70+ people in our company in addition to all the other guests who saw it, praying for their need! That is powerful, and this happens at the beginning of your service. Do you think the tone is set for your experience? I believe that you can create any type of environment you want as long as you are willing to think it through! Sometimes, it is a contest; other times, it is simply creating interaction with your crew. Whatever VIBE you want, get excited because now you have the ability to create it.

Systems Based Success

I think you knew this was coming and as we wrap up this indicator, you must always realize that *anything can be systematized to create a more direct result.* (Was that just an unidentified nugget? You choose.) So many people feel that their finances, technical ability, fitness, diet and many other things can be regimented to create success and that the VIBE of an environment just happens. This couldn't be further from the truth.

As I told you earlier, when I started our company eleven years ago, I wanted to have everyone on the same page. So I set a meeting every week at the same time. Every week, each team member was responsible for sharing who inspired them, and it had to be specific. This was a deliberate system to manipulate the Vibe in our environment! Today, we have over 70 employees, and the VIBE across all of our locations is to find people doing something right! Coincidence? You know the answer to that one. Are you feeling me?

Once you realize that *Happy* isn't always the answer, you can choose the way you want to be viewed internally and externally. Asking yourself the question, "How can I manipulate the vibe in my environment?" will ultimately help you to create systems that will sustain a consistent vibe that will adapt to the needs of the present. Vibe is something that can be manipulated but never forced. You must think about this from a farmer's mentality—seed time and harvest. Creating the proper vibe is a metaphor of life—identify the crop, prepare the soil, plant the seed, water, and patiently wait for the harvest!

Please take the time now to write out 5 different vibes that would be advantageous to your environment.

....

....

....

....

....

Specifically, target how you want to be viewed internally and externally:

....

....

....

....

....

....

List out 7 Vibe manipulators that you can use: (Be creative and make sure that they make you smile.)

....

....

....

....

....

....

Based on these last three exercises, what systems can you put in place to ensure your desired result:

....

....

....

....

....

....

Score yourself on a scale of 1–10 based on your personal vibe and your ability to create a positive vibe in others:

Circle One:

1   2   3   4   5   6   7   8   9   10

INDICATOR #2 NUGGETS

Anytime you try to create only one exclusive VIBE,
you run the risk of alienating a larger percentage
of your crew!

If you want to improve an area of your environment,
simply change the vibe!

True customer service is nothing more than a byproduct
of authentic relationships between the team members of
the organization or company.

You must be specific and deliberate with your intentions
to get the desired result in anything that you do.

Uninhibited constant communication
will break down all walls.

Too much of one thing can kill the desire for it.

A manager will react to the vibe of their environment,
but a leader will create systems that will
deliver their desired Vibe.

PROCESS (PROCEDURE)

proc·ess[21]

ˈprä͜ses,ˈprō͜ses/

noun

noun: **process**; plural noun: **processes**

1. a series of actions or steps taken in order to achieve a particular end.

pro·ce·dure[22]

prəˈsējər/

noun

noun: **procedure**; plural noun: **procedures**

1. an established or official way of doing something.

Rules without relationship will cause rebellion.

I was in Columbus, Ohio, a beautiful city, doing a hair show (GO WARRIORS). The morning started off great— the models were beautiful, the prep room was buzzing with

21   https://en.oxforddictionaries.com/definition/process
22   https://en.oxforddictionaries.com/definition/procedure

energy, and everything seemed to be going according to plan. In spite of all this, something seemed to be off…I could feel it in the air. Have you ever had the feeling that something is amiss, but you cannot seem to put your finger on it? I assessed the environment and went through my mental checklist: models✔, supplies✔, music✔, team…

Aha, that was it. It was something to do with my team. And then it hit me like a ton of bricks. Sara Bryan, now the VP of our company, seemed a little shorter that morning. In all the time that I knew Sara, she was a force when she walked into the room. Standing at 5'7", she owned every environment that she ever entered. To be honest, I don't think that I had ever seen her in flat shoes. This particular morning, her shoes were not only flat but so was her presence. It was the strangest thing. Her confidence was at an all-time low. This superhero had encountered her Kryptonite, and it was in the form of a pair of shoes that kept her low to the ground. I pulled her into the hall and asked what was going on? She looked at me as if to say I feel it too but I cannot identify what is causing it. I shared with her that I knew what the challenge was. She was excited to hear my insight. I immediately pointed to the shoes that she was wearing and let her know that everything that morning was the same except for her flat shoes, she didn't own the room like she normally did! We laughed it off and made a pact that she would never wear low shoes again in a professional environment because she is a superstar who makes an incredible impact. To this day, I have never been in a working environment with Sara where she didn't command the room!

After a couple of years, Sara and I never really thought about this again until it was brought up in a class that I was teaching. A young lady raised her hand and said that she wanted to work with our company, but her friends told her that she should let go of that desire because I force all the women in my company to wear high heels every day and she didn't think she could do that. As you can imagine, I was floored by this statement. Where had this come from? And then my memory engaged. This young lady must have heard about Sara in Columbus. I chuckled inside, and then I took the time to explain that particular situation only applied to Sara. I also explained that if the only way you can own a room or feel like your most powerful self is by wearing high heels, then sleep in those bad-boys! On the other hand, if you can control your environment wearing flats, then more power to you. I believe that we all know what gives us our Swag. (If you don't, take the time now to put down this book and identify it.) Now we are on the same page. Once you identify this, then the key is to apply it!

NUGGET:

Knowledge without application is dead!

If you feel great when you wear black, then wear black! If you feel sexy when your makeup is done, then do your makeup…Always. This was the lesson with the reason **why** accompanying it. When a rule is in place but there is no relationship connected, there is going to be trouble.

People have no problem following you when you know exactly where you are going (or seem like it)!

"Lack of clear vision will destroy hope!"

Hope is something that needs to be protected at all costs because it is very hard if not impossible to repair. I believe that hope is in the details of processes and procedures. They make people feel safe because they know what to expect. Fixing a broken light bulb, or unclogging a drain, these things can be monumental when it comes to establishing hope. They say that the devil is in the details, but I think that is where Jesus lays His hat. Boom!

NUGGET:

Make sure that when something breaks in your work environment, you get it fixed as soon as supernaturally (I think this is better than humanly) possible! This will prove to be a foundational building block of hope!

It's not only things that are broken that can decay hope. Misused words, contradictory actions, profanity, social media posts, or a plethora of other things also have the same effect. This is where open communication will prove to be your greatest ally. You don't have to be perfect or even close. Just make sure that you are swift in making things better... Got it? Good!

Resting Places

Steve and Terri Cowan[23] are two of the most dynamic speakers that I have ever experienced. They once came to a business that I was working with and told us that we were better from a distance than we were up close. I had never been kicked in the teeth (figuratively) and loved it so much. I was blessed to spend a weekend with them, and I was overwhelmed by their wisdom and the ability to translate it to all who encountered them. One of the millions of nuggets that I took away from this experience was that everything has a resting place! Let's take a second and think if you applied

---

23   http://www.professionalsalonconcepts.com/terri-steve-cowan/

this to your kids' bedroom.

Just hear me out on this one…Go into your child's bedroom and clean it to look exactly the way you'd love to see it every day. Take out your phone and take pictures of every angle that you can think of (just like you were posting it on Zillow). Now, you can go old school and print them out, or you can create a digital folder. Even better yet, prepare a keynote presentation complete with music! Under each photo, list out everything you see, leave nothing to chance. Explain in detail exactly what you see and how to accomplish the task. After you have done this, schedule a time to present it to your children! Make it fun, pop popcorn, maybe even dim the lights. Take them through the experience and open it up to questions. Make sure that each and every task is listed and explained so that everyone is on the same page. Then and only then can you hold them accountable!

So many of us deal with frustration over things not being the way that we want them. Imagine if you applied this technique to all areas of your business, it would change the game! Resting places—this isn't only about physical things, this can apply to mentality too. How do you want your work environment to feel, function and operate? Take some time and ponder this for a second. You can move the needle in any way you want it to go as long as you are willing to clearly communicate your goal (and sometimes sprinkle sugar on top of it!). I have goose bumps as I am writing this and I hope that I am not the only one!

In your physical environment, you can simply set it up exactly the way you want it and explain it in a caption that is engaging and create a standard that will be carried out devoid of any emotion. This will not happen overnight, though. It takes time and discipline, but then again, doesn't everything that has value take time? Mentally, try to keep resting places for when you wake up. Try keeping a positive book near your bed that you read immediately when you wake up and before you go to bed. If you want to be more fit, have a book on fitness on the night stand...Do you see it? Resting places are nothing more than a road map that clearly communicates where things need to go once they are used! I think that there might be some nuggets hidden around here!

Steve and Terri introduced me to this concept, and it shook me to the core. We immediately used this in our business, and it took away the excuse (that I always used), "I didn't know where it went, that is why I didn't clean up!" This created many different effects in our workplace. It made people feel safe, confident, competent, and to tell you the truth, it enhanced our SWAG! People started having a sense of accomplishment when they could put the place back together quickly and efficiently. My Pops always tells me that you gain competence, confidence and then you cop an attitude. This is exactly what happens when you give people the tools to succeed, and then you sprinkle a little bit of magic on it called *Public Praise*. These pages must be hot in your hand because I am dropping fire right now! (It's OK to laugh. That way, the person sitting next to you will ask you what you are reading, and you will have the opportunity to share with them something that will change their life! You are already making a difference, and you aren't even done with this book. GREAT WORK!)

Not Only What You Do
But Also Why You Do Them

Every process and procedure needs to have a relatable story attached to it that will give it life!

I love the Four Seasons Hotel,[24] and I love staying there and justifying it as research. Remember, when we said that sweet Jesus was in the details? Well, this company is the highest level example of this theory. People who work with the Four Seasons own the story behind every process and procedure that they execute on a daily basis.

We were staying in Maui[25] and I wanted to test this. Earlier in the day, I was in the lobby, and there was the most delightful lemonade tea mixture that I had ever experienced. Alright, simmer down, you are saying in your head, "You mean an Arnold Palmer[26] that you can get anywhere?" No. I am talking about a drink that I still talk about 11 years

---

24   https://www.fourseasons.com/
25   http://www.fourseasons.com/maui/
26   http://www.arnoldpalmer.com/beverages

later. On top of all this, it is only served in the lobby from 12 noon–3 pm. Fast forward to about 11 pm. We were in our room, and I told my beautiful, loving, compassionate, intelligent wife that I was thirsty and wanted that tea. She responded the same way any loving wife would by saying, "Are you kidding me? It's 11 pm. Drink some tap water and go to bed!"

Although listening to your wife is a great thing, I chose, just this one time, to chase my desire for the Tea that was dropped straight from heaven. I called down to the lobby and asked for *The Tea*, and quickly there was a knock at our door. I opened the door, but to my surprise they had simply delivered regular Lipton tea. At this point, my wife told me to just drink the tea and be happy…this was only the second time that I thought it was OK to follow my dream in spite of her trying to crush it. I reached for the phone, and she tried to slap it out of my hand. But my three months of Taekwondo training when I was 8 kicked in and my reflexes were too fast. The operator answered, and I explained my desire for the **Tea from Heaven**. Surprisingly, she not only had it delivered but also had the recipe printed out so I could recreate this masterpiece! You see, the Four Seasons company empowers their team to have an unlimited budget to make people happy no matter what position they hold in the company! They understand that the processes they utilize to create success must always have life.

As mentioned earlier, everything has a **why** attached to it and as long as that is clear, almost everything else will fall in line. There will always be human error, but that is what the spice of life is. In every successful relationship or business I have encountered, there are systems in play that help to build the organization or personal bond. For instance, date night is something that my wife and I look forward to and has become a system with a reason **why** attached to it.

We were at church in Chicago where I had the opportunity to be a guest speaker. The pastor had invited us into his office before the service started and gave my wife and me some advice that really changed the landscape of our marriage. He was talking about his routine at home, and he glazed over the fact that his kids went to bed at 7 p.m. Both my wife and I stopped him in mid-conversation and asked him to confirm his outlandish claim. He then repeated that his kids went to bed at 7 p.m.! As new parents of two children, we were struggling to get our kids to bed at any decent hour, so we inquired how this was even possible. The pastor leaned in, paused and said, "My wife and I agreed that it was better to be disciplined and put them to bed at 7 p.m., rather than them waking up to their step-parents!" Silence covered the room as we pondered the meaning of this. The pastor broke the silence by saying that he and his wife needed **their time**. I am sure you know what I mean? Imagine the implications. The kids have a specific bedtime, and the parents now get to shift roles and be husband and wife. That's what I am talking about! This will give the couple time to communicate, solve challenges, and express their dreams and aspirations among other things—ultimately laying the foundation for a healthy life.

NUGGET:

When the reason why is strong enough, it will become second nature.

Think about this in your business life. Whenever you have a process or procedure that is linked to the end vision, it becomes an invaluable part of the operation.

Processes and Procedures are Nothing More Than a List of Your Screw-Ups!

We started this one off with a nugget. Imagine if everyone in your organization understood that all of the rules and regulations were in place because somebody messed up and you want to make sure that they have a better existence. This creates the freedom to make mistakes as long as we are committed to making it better for the customers.

How many of you who have kids have ever given them ice cream right before bedtime? My single people, how many of you have ever overextended yourself financially (only because you deserved it?) only to come up short on your bills.

Business professionals, have you ever made a bad decision that cost you dearly? Well, if you can relate to any or all of this, then this concept can make a difference for you. People used to always say to me, "Chalk it up to experience!" I believe we can forget the chalk and write it down to become a part of our procedure DNA! Take a second and think about the top 5 screw-ups in your life…Would you ever want to have them happen again? Yes, the lessons are valuable, no one is disputing that. What I am saying is that the implementation of that knowledge can create streamlined success in your future!

One of the leaders in our Reservations Department at the Hard Rock Salon[27] in Vegas took on the task of coordinating an event that we were doing. Although it was her first time doing something of this magnitude, she took it on with such focus and attention to detail that the event ran very smoothly except for a couple of areas that caused challenges. The first one was that our team had a couple of drinks at the event, nothing major. However, this is something that is a non-negotiable in our culture although this particular night, there was a curve ball thrown our team's way. My new partner who hadn't been a part of our culture long enough didn't know about our *non-drinking at events* policy. I was emailed immediately that night by the organizer of the event to let me know that as a vendor, there was to be no drinking at

27   https://hardrockhotel.com/las-vegas-amenities/kelly-cardenas-salon.php

all because this was a hospitality area for invited guests and the alcohol was for them and them only. Point taken. We screwed up but it wasn't the end of the world.

The second instance was, I believe, connected with the first one. When we were loading out of the event, a couple of things happened that were very unfortunate. But because of the alcohol incident, they were blown way out of proportion. In most cases, a person would lose their ability to coordinate events in the future or based off the severity, be relieved from their duty. Our *culture* is based on the fact that "Rules are nothing more than a list of your screw ups." So our process is simply to learn from it and make it better.

You will be glad to know that in the following year, we had a couple of **new** procedures (rules) in place. I also had the same young lady head up the event and this year, her execution was flawless. We actually had her correspond with the company that we were working with through an alternate email, so she wouldn't deal with preconceived notions. Her attention to detail was unmatched and she was so engaged with every detail, translating to her team at every moment not only what to do but also why they were doing it. This year's event was done by the same exact people as the year before, and the heads of the organization came to me and thanked me for how amazing our crew and all the communication had been leading up to the event. Little did they know that they were dealing with the same crew member from the previous year. In this case, we learned two valuable lessons. The first: Certain actions can cause people to assume things about you that you may not intend. The second: When you are given the permission to screw-up, as long as you are willing to make it better, you experience the freedom to unlock your potential. The young lady's name is Lauren[28] and I am so proud of her resilience. She is now the premiere coordinator of events in our whole company, and people know that when she is on the task, we are set up for success. As a company or human being, you will never be perfect. This is a silly expectation of people and ourselves. So make as many mistakes as you want today. Just commit to making things better and then write them down so the next person can avoid making the mistakes you made!

I have messed up so many times in my life, and I have been fortunate enough to be given enough grace to work through it. I thank God for these people not giving up on me.

I get asked all the time from people trying to improve their businesses, "What do I need to do to get what I want?" Whether that be more profit, a better culture, an enhanced environment or more efficiency, my answer is always the same…Start by listing all of your screw-ups and give your people the ability to mess up as long as they are willing to make it better! This kind of environment will prove to be

---

28   https://www.kellycardenassalon.com/team/lauren-hoggan

more productive, efficient and profitable, not to mention enjoyable simply because your people will own and be engaged with the process and procedures. Your team will foster a sense of freedom in them as opposed to feeling controlled.

As we wrap up this chapter, please know that **Rules without relationship will cause rebellion**. Also, lack of vision will destroy hope. And finally, identifying the Resting place in your business is at the core of all processes and procedures. Helping your people to understand the **why** will breathe life into everything that you do and knowing that **Rules are nothing more than a list of your screw-ups** will provide the freedom that people need to unlock their potential!

Now, take a minute and think of **3** things that you can create resting places for—one in your personal, one in your business, and one in your mentality. Take a picture of the business and personal and you will have to draw a picture of your mentality. Think of 5 procedures that you have and list out the reason WHY they are in place.

....

....

....

....

....

I would also like you to list any screw-ups that came from these procedures.

Don't worry, we won't judge!

....
....
....
....
....

Score yourself on a scale of 1–10 based on your awareness and creation of a healthy culture:

<u>Circle One:</u>

1   2   3   4   5   6   7   8   9   10

INDICATOR #3 NUGGETS

Knowledge without application is dead!

Make sure that when something breaks in your work environment, you get it fixed as soon as supernaturally (I think this is better than humanly) possible! This will prove to be a foundational building block of hope!

**When the reason why is strong enough,
it will become second nature.**

PRODUCTIVITY

pro·duc·tiv·I·ty[29]
/ˌprōˌdəkˈtivədē, ˌprädəkˈtivədē/
noun

the effectiveness of productive effort, especially in industry, as measured in terms of the rate of output per
unit of input.

"workers have boosted productivity by 30 percent"

synonyms:

efficiency, work rate;

When I was in 4th grade, my Pops did something that
he will never live down. It changed all of our lives, stretched
our thinking, made us mad, almost put us in the poor house,
and nearly landed my Pops in prison. Although it did create
principles for hard work dedication, a road map for business
and life, while taking three knucklehead kids and turning
them into a doctor, one of the top attorneys in the country
and a dreamer turned entrepreneur!

---

29   https://en.oxforddictionaries.com/definition/productivity

That something was called "The Course." I remember my Pops coming home so excited—it was as if he'd found the magic beans! "The Course" in a nutshell was:

A training program that taught you how to be a millionaire by selling this course to others so they could learn how to be a millionaire also…did I just lose you? I spoke in a circle on purpose to help you understand the concept. Yes, it was a pyramid scheme at its finest, or so I thought. That is, until later in my life, when I realized the results. Most of us don't spend time on our filter; we just rely on our eyesight. This is not a bad way to live. Your eyesight can evaluate challenges up ahead and help you to avoid challenges before they hit. On the flip side, your filter, if you have invested in it, can help you sift through some of life's greatest blows to find the nugget of gold that lies in wait.

Your filter will allow you to look on the bright side of every circumstance because you know that there is a silver lining. I really don't believe that this is putting your head in the sand, rather creating an optimistic outlook on anything that comes your way. I learned a lot about my filter from my parents. My Pops would always encourage us to fall in love with what we had as opposed to desiring all the things we didn't. My Mom was what we call **Macgyver** in the kitchen. She could take anything, including potato chips, and make a casserole. So throughout my childhood, my parents would not only tell us this, they would embody it themselves through the way they viewed their situation. Do you understand the concept of your Filter?…Good.

Back to "The Course." Each day after school, my brother and I had to take ten pages of notes before we could go out and play. Now, this is where my brother started to get upset with me. My Big Brother Rob had nice handwriting, and up until then, that was an attribute he was rewarded for. Mine, on the other hand, looked like a five-year-old was attempting to write with his feet. I was always given grief from my schoolmates and teachers. Little did I know it would be advantageous to me. My brother's nice and neat handwriting took up very little space, and my chicken scratch only allowed about 5 words per line. To add insult to injury, I skipped lines in between each sentence. This enabled me to complete my assignment and be out playing in no time!

NUGGET:

When you fall in love with your shortcomings, they will prove to be some of your greatest strengths.

Another task that was introduced to our family by "The Course" was that my brother and I were required to get 100 "ships" ready to go out every Saturday before we mowed three lawns and then we could go out and play. A "ship" was a cassette tape on which we had to write my Pop's name, our address, and our 1-800 number and extension. You can imagine how small that writing had to be. My brother and I would try and have as much fun in the process that we could. But most of our conversation was about how when we grew up, we would never do this to our kids! There were many more tasks incited by "The Course," but I think you get the idea!

Why am I telling you this and what does it have to do with the title of this Chapter? Great question. So here we go!

NUGGET:

You cannot argue with results!

Now, I am not condoning stepping outside of principle merely to get results. I am saying that sometimes we don't see the end game. We see only the non-favorable circumstances at the time. When our filter is strong, we can work through life's craziness with the understanding that something great is going to come out of it. All of the notes and "ships" that we filled out were a way for my brother and I to learn discipline, focus, task-orientated success, as well as all of the incredible principles that were in "The Course." At face value, it was a pyramid scheme created to take money from people, but as we filtered it, it proved to be the foundation of my brothers' and my success. This story only has validity because of the results of our careers and lives. Without the proof of Productivity, these theories are empty words!

We Must Have Concrete Stories of Success in Our Immediate Environment

I received a call that offered me my dream job in San Diego. This was something that I had sought out for over 2½ years. I was ecstatic that my dreams were now my reality. Although I was given the opportunity of a lifetime, there were also sacrifices and concessions that I was going to have to make in order to seize the opportunity. The first was moving away from my parents' house in Memphis to San Diego, one of the most beautiful and expensive places to live in the US.

NUGGET:

Opportunity will generally come wrapped in something that is not desirable.

When I arrived, I was instantly indoctrinated into the stories of success that the team has experienced. This gave me hope, helped me to see past the day, and enabled me to see a future in my new endeavor.

One story stuck out to me and helped to shape me in my career. The whole team at different times spoke of a legendary day of production as if it was their own. It actually belonged to my boss. It was a $1600 day. One hairdresser had done $1600 in service in one day. I was blown away every time I heard it, although the more it entered my ears, the closer it moved toward my heart and ultimately became my reality! What really solidified it was when Robert (my boss) corroborated the tale. I was the lucky one that he chose to travel with him to a hair show. And although I was honored to work with him onstage, I soon learned that the real magic happened on the plane ride there and back.

NUGGET:

The end game is sweet, but it is in the journey where the magic is!

As we sat down on the plane, Robert began to tell me stories of his adventures all over the world and of times that were priceless to him. As he told me these stories, he got all excited. It was almost as if he was getting the opportunity to re-live these amazing memories. I thought for a second that he was enjoying this more than me and then I remembered that I had dreamed of this moment for over three years,08[So I was definitely the lucky one! As he told me about his storied career, I secretly hoped that he would tell the story of the $1600 day. It was about an hour and a half into the flight when he started in on the story! My heart sang, *It was true.* It was true, and because I work by his side and in his system, it can be my reality also! This fueled me, and when I had a day with not one guest (a $0 day), I whisked my mind away to the day when I was doing $1600! This kept my spirits high!

In every environment, we must have stories of success that are regularly spoken about. This will create and sustain hope. Something as simple as posting performance on a weekly or monthly basis can change the landscape. Most people leave companies for the simple fact that they don't see a future. Paint a clear picture of it and make it a part of your culture to discuss and celebrate the successes that they are a part of. I would suggest doing this *monthly* and when you see the amazing results, then do it *weekly*. Your environment will catch fire, and you will contemplate doing it *daily*. In our company, not a week goes by without someone surpassing a record that is company wide or a personal best of theirs.

I learned this through a challenge that I set for myself. One day, I decided to face my fear of running. The first day, I intended to make it as far as I could go, which was the end of my block (don't judge). As I crept closer to the corner, I set my sights on a car about half a block away. My mind started to stretch and before I knew it, I was halfway around the neighborhood. At this point, I made up my mind to complete the mile loop because I figured: *Since I had gone this far, I might as well complete the task.* This led to an expanded mindset about my capacity to run. Once I was aware that it was possible, I started to talk with my friends about how far they had run and how fast they had done it. The more I looked into it, the more I realized what was possible if I was willing to put in the work.

NUGGET

You need to know what is possible and you need to have something you can aspire to accomplish.

Best Days and Best Weeks

We go as far as to publish the best days and best weeks of all of our team members. This is something that I see as crucial although I catch a lot of flak for it when I bring it up to other cultures. I completely understand why they are resistant. People have cited that it will cause division and a negative environment. But in my experience, I have found exactly the opposite to be true. We just had an experience in our company that was eye opening. We had a director's retreat about two years ago, and we set goals for the following year. Well, these goals ended up out of sight until a week ago. As I read through them, I realized that almost every one of them had been accomplished. The challenge, however, was that they had *not* been celebrated.

NUGGET:

A goal fulfilled that is not celebrated has about the same value as one not set.

When I shared these goals with our leadership crew, they were surprised and excited—not only about the ones they had accomplished, but also they were motivated to set new ones to target. This time though we will be sure to celebrate them. From the wise words of **Kool & the Gang**, "Celebrate good times, come on!"[30]

In our culture, it was something that was done from the beginning, and I have seen unity and healthy competition (with one's self). I am not telling you that this is a must. I am just speaking from my experience. When a new kid enters our company and hears about a person doing $10,500 in service in one week, that becomes their reality. When we simply write things down, they become attainable by all of those who encounter it.

NUGGET:

If you want something to become a part of your culture and continually grow, focus on it and celebrate it publicly!

---

30   https://en.wikipedia.org/wiki/Celebration_(Kool_%26_the_Gang_song)

What are Your Leaders Doing?

Once you start to emphasize the productivity of your crew, they will start to ask about the leader's production. I know that this sounds backward but I needed you to warm up to the concept of reporting your performance first, and then we can add this element. I believe that you can always take a quick snapshot of a company or family simply by looking at the productivity of the leaders!

I am blessed to be able to volunteer at my daughter's school, and whenever I see good or bad behavior in her classmates, it is almost always a reflection of the leadership in their household. The same thing rings true for the performance of any team. As I once heard famously in the movie *Remember the Titans*,[31] "Attitude always reflects leadership."

People look at the performance of those who lead them. In any organization or family, the simple way to assess the environment is to look at what the leaders are doing. When leaders rise, they bring the whole organization with them. Now, I believe that a true leader will train people to be better than they ever were. And when we look into the implications of this, the sum of what they create through others cannot be touched by any one individual. So effectively, they will still be producing on a higher level.

---

31   https://en.wikipedia.org/wiki/Remember_the_Titans

NUGGET:

My Pops always told me, "It's not about what you can do but what you can get done through others!"

In a lot of environments, the leaders think they are immune and in some cases, above the details that make up the foundation of the organization. I like to emphasize the opposite. Although there are certain perks that leaders enjoy, they must adhere strictly to the principles of the organization that they lead. Your leader's **Productivity** is at the core of all of this! If you want a quick snapshot of your business, simply turn your focus on to what your leaders are doing. If you find that your leaders are *not* performing, the team is most likely to follow suit. However, if your leaders are excelling and the people are deficient, then you may discover that they are not leaders after all.

Have They Maximized by Your Systems?

As we were just speaking about the productivity of the leaders in your organization or family, we must look to see if they have been maximized by the systems at play in our culture.

When we started our company, one of the first things that I wanted to get in line was having the right accountant. This was the advice that I had been given multiple times through multiple sources. When I finally met with my accountant, she assured me that I had made the right decision, because it was better to set things on the right path from the beginning rather than have to fix it down the line. I knew that I wanted to have the best in the business at their respective discipline to enable me to focus on what I was good at. I set a system in place that would help to maximize my potential. Another thing that I was adamant about was to create systems that allowed the magic of my people to shine. I worked hard to create an environment that would amplify my people's strengths and create a safe place for them to work through their weakness. Now, this can only happen when you give your people the freedom and confidence to audit the process constantly.

As a result, we developed the ability to change things on the fly, try new ideas, and test out crazy ideas that might prove to be some of the greatest that we have ever had. We quickly adopt a concept along these lines: if it works, then we break it down, systematize it and make it a part of our culture or if it sucks, we stop doing it.

To truly maximize people, you must understand who they are and what their strengths consist of. I have almost made a career out of putting people in the wrong position and then wondering why they aren't performing. I once had a young lady who was one of the greatest technicians that I had ever seen. And because of that, I put her in a leadership position that emphasized communication, and I watched her decline. This was my fault. Instead of maximizing her strengths by putting her into education or simply allowing her greatness to shine, I assumed that it would translate to all other aspects of our business. This doesn't apply only to leadership or business but to all areas of life. You must get to know people and help to build structures around them that will help them to ascend.

Are Your Systems Designed for High Performance?

I was so excited to move to San Diego although I had no idea what was in store. I walked into an environment that consisted of two schedules for one person and three dedicated support staff members allocated to ensure high-level service. I was blown away. That's how it was, I didn't have a choice. It was like getting nudged off the cliff into the water below. Halfway down, you cannot decide that you don't want to get wet. This became my reality. I adapted to it and started to think of ways that it could be maximized further.

I believe this is how life works—we stretch and grow, and then repeat the process. I work with a woman named Jenn,[32] and she is a high-performance person in all that she does. Yes, she is one of those…I know that not everyone is going to push themselves the way she does and that is exactly why I build systems to level the playing field. I want people to be able to realize their potential and experience the simplicity of

---

32   https://www.kellycardenassalon.com/team/jenn-moses

working in a system that is designed for high performance. No matter who they are or where they come from, they can experience growth that is simply unimaginable.

My friend Nando[33] once told me that he had no real goals. He said that he'd be OK with simply paying his bills. These days, I often refer to him as the most successful person in our company not because he produces the most but because how far he has come in relation to where he started. High-performance systems are going to be relative to the starting point of the individual. Please don't get caught up, like me, in the early stages of my career. I had the wrong notion that everyone should be held to one standard. Your systems must have legs meaning that you take into account the unmeasurable aspects of growth within the individual.

NUGGET:

If your systems aren't built for high performance, you cannot expect high-level results, and if they do happen, there is no structure in place to sustain them.

Most people react to high-level performance as opposed to setting out with that expectation. I would urge you to take some time right now and look at the systems in your company or relationship and ask yourself if they are built for high performance.

---

33   https://www.kellycardenassalon.com/team/fernando-adame

Productivity must be measured, written down, displayed, and celebrated publicly to make it a part of your culture. Concrete stories of success will create and sustain hope in your organization. Celebrating best practices will help to cultivate more of the same, and will create a focal point on your leader's performance. This being said, it is imperative that your leaders are maximized by the systems you have in place. Finally, you must constantly evaluate your environment to ensure it is designed for high performance.

Now is the time to write down 3 of the largest success stories in your company.

....

....

....

....

....

....

What are some measurable results that you can list and begin to track and celebrate publicly?

....

....

....

....

....

Write down 3 of your leader's success stories.

....

....

....

....

....

....

Write down 5 systems that you implement that were built for high performance.

....

....

....

....

....

....

Finally, write out 3 stories of people who have had amazing success that cannot be measured by traditional numbers. Once you do this, go and celebrate these three people publicly in your business or family and watch the Magic happen.

....

....

....

....

....

Score yourself on a scale of 1–10 based on your productivity:

Circle One:

1   2   3   4   5   6   7   8   9   10

INDICATOR #4 NUGGETS

When you fall in love with your shortcomings, they will prove to be some of your greatest strengths.

You cannot argue with results!

Opportunity will generally come wrapped in something that is not desirable.

The end game is sweet, but it is in the journey where the magic is!

You need to know what is possible and you need to have something you can aspire to accomplish.

A goal fulfilled that is not celebrated has about
the same value as one not set.

If you want something to become a part of
your culture and continually grow, focus on it
and celebrate it publicly!

My Pops always told me, "It's not about what you
can do but what you can get done through others!"

If your systems aren't built for high performance, you
cannot expect high-level results, and if they do happen,
there is no structure in place to sustain them.

Indicator #5

Innovation

in·no·va·tion[34]
/ˌinəˈvāSH(ə)n/
noun
noun: **innovation**

1 the action or process of innovating.

2 synonyms:

3 change, alteration, revolution, upheaval, transformation, metamorphosis, breakthrough; More new measures, new methods, modernization, novelty, newness;

creativity, originality, ingenuity, inspiration, inventiveness;

informal a shake up

"no appliance manufacturer can survive without an ongoing commitment to innovation"

---

34   http://innovate365.co/index.html

When we were growing up, my Pops was the kind of guy who could do anything. He knew how to fix the car, do drywall, paint the house, fix my bike, and even play ping-pong. You could call him a renaissance man if you will. I believe that his spirit of innovation came largely from desperation. As a kid, I watched him invent new ways to accomplish his goals simply because we didn't have the money to buy the solution. I love this way of thinking, and I have tried to use it in every area of my business and life. One of my favorite instances was when I was in 5th grade. My Pops bought dog clippers so that we could save money by shaving the dog ourselves. Although this proved to be one of the hardest things that you can do with a dog, it spawned an adventure that would change my life. After one failed try, we put the clippers underneath the sink for about 3–4 years. That is until one day I needed a haircut and my big brother Rob offered his services while my oldest brother watched and laughed. Little did I know that day would be the beginning of my journey in the professional beauty industry.

Innovation to me is what happens when you are free to try out new things. When you see a challenge and create a solution, your confidence skyrockets.

NUGGET:

Your challenges are just opportunities to create unique solutions. Your business and relationships must embrace Innovation to have the ability to grow.

Innovation is always at the core of anything successful.

Sometimes Money Will Dull Your Creativity

I learned this from my friend Dave during Christmas one year. I was flying out to Las Vegas to see him, and for the first time in my life, I was making enough money to be able to buy him pretty much whatever I wanted at the time. I am not talking Bentleys and Yachts—I am talking a CD and a shirt from Merry-go-round. I went nuts in my mind and bought him everything that I could think of. I wrapped them all nicely with the best paper and was so excited to arrive at his house to deliver the spoils. Immediately upon arrival, I wanted to exchange gifts, thinking that I would blow him away with my grandiose nature. When the moment I looked forward to so much finally arrived, Dave stunned me. He actually handed me his gift first. As I peeled back the wrapping, I wanted to not only return all of the gifts that I had bought, but I also wanted to crawl into a hole and never come out. When all the wrapping paper was gone, I was face to face with not only one of the greatest gifts that I'd ever received, but I also learned a lesson that would live in my heart forever! His gift was a frame with about 6–7 pictures of him and me at different memorable times in our lives. He gave from his heart, and I gave from my wallet. Dave's method will prove to be a winner in all aspects of life while mine will create only a temporary feeling of happiness.

Don't fall into the trap of thinking that just because you can throw money at a challenge, you should. Now, there are always times when we have to spend top dollar to get the best. This is referred to as *the cost of doing business*. I have learned over the years that the ability to decipher between the two will be of huge importance. Innovation is not just about spending money, and it's definitely not cutting corners. It's about creating a culture where people have bought in and own the vision. So much so, they are willing to challenge the status quo to improve the landscape for all involved. The more and more success you enjoy, the more important it is for true innovation to be a part of your DNA. I love to hear the stories of desperation that end up becoming a procedure that cannot be lived without. For every 10–20 ideas, one will stick and that is alright! You must take time to celebrate the **one** that worked as opposed to wasting time talking about the ones that did not work.

NUGGET

If it Works, Break it Down and Systematize it; If it Sucks Don't Use it Anymore!

I spoke of this theory earlier, and I want to stress the importance of people having the freedom, better yet, being excited about having new ideas. Winn Claybaugh[35] always says the 6 words that can kill any culture are, "We've always done it that way." The very core of any healthy culture depends on their ability to innovate.

Eli Winters,[36] our director in Chicago, once took her weekend off to organize and paint the backroom. Her reasoning was that she wanted her team to experience joy and relaxation when they entered. She knows how hard her crew works and the organization would simplify their work day and the bright yellow wall would bring sunshine into their heart. Now, she was not paid for this. She identified an area that could be improved, and she acted.

Eli Atkins[37] works with us in Vegas, and he came up with a spreadsheet that would enable our directors to have a quick snapshot of the week's performance based on a few key indicators. Selena Arreguin[38] works with us in Chicago and created a Streamlined **"Where you at?"** template to help us

---

35 http://www.retail-merchandiser.com/7-print/featured-content/564-the-paul-mitchell-schools
36 https://www.kellycardenassalon.com/team/eli-winters
37 https://www.kellycardenassalon.com/team/eli-atkins
38 https://www.kellycardenassalon.com/team/selena-arreguin

stay in touch with all of our team members and let us know where they are at in all aspects of their lives. Sara Bryan created **The Foil Box** that has become not only a staple in our company but in the professional beauty industry. Kelsey Fenner[39] became the first stylist to prove that our system can adapt to any injury. Kelsey started having challenges with her wrist, the perpetual movement of being a hairdresser was creating immense pain. Her doctor finally told her that she was going to have to find another profession. I chose not to believe that diagnosis and with my extensive medical background (watching numerous movies about doctors and my 12th grade education), I chose to put on my "rose-colored glasses." We assessed what actions were causing her pain and then assigned an assistant to her to take care of all the aspects of her business that were contributing to this. The result is a kid in our assistant program who has the opportunity to learn and grow from one of the most brilliant minds in our industry. Not to mention developing an *industry first system* that will enable anyone with any injury to continue doing what they love regardless of their condition. Kelsey has since doubled her production, mentored young hairdressers, and completely changed her perspective about her limitations.

---

39   https://www.kellycardenassalon.com/team/kelsey-fenner

Other Innovations in Our Company

My beautiful wife[40] created a full-service concierge business for weddings kcsweddings.com. We created our own set of scissors[41] that would standardize cutting across the nation in our salons. We came up with what we call weekly synopsis where each of our directors writes out and posts to our team Facebook page all of the celebrations that happened during the week. They list specific people and instances that happened in their location. Some have even incorporated videos to match people doing things right. Bobby Bosch[42] in our Chicago location pours his heart and soul into his synopsis every week, so much so that people that aren't even named engage with his posts! He adds humor, passion, and of course, the secret sauce of his personality to every aspect of his writing.

These are just a couple examples of the innovation in our company. I believe that you should think about your culture as a living breathing organism—ever changing, with new needs and desires all the time.

I think of it like my children. My son Maddox is 5, and he is wide open! "Play baseball with me Dad, let's play soccer, climb a tree, ride my ziggle-ziggle bike, play Legos"— and all this before lunch. Just two years ago, he was content

---

40   https://www.kellycardenassalon.com/team/brooklyn-cardenas
41   https://www.shiroshears.com/products/kelly-cardenas-collection/
42   https://www.kellycardenassalon.com/team/bobby-bosch

with snuggling up and watching a movie with me.

People grow and so should our cultures. They evolve and are in need of constant innovation. You don't have to make monumental shifts as long as you continue to make progress. Innovation in its simplest form is to be yourself and have fun with what you are doing. This will cause you to look at things with the perspective that always keeps things fresh. Remember, money can dull your creativity. So create a culture from the start that will intertwine the practice of innovation throughout your organization.

I would love for you to write down 5 examples where Money has dulled your creativity.

....

....

....

....

....

....

This week, I want you to celebrate someone for just having an idea, whether it is good or not doesn't matter.

....

....

....

....

Finally, I want you to identify an idea that you have had that worked. Break it down to the lowest common denominator and systematize it.

....

....

....

....

....

....

I also want you to write out an idea that sucked and share it with your colleagues.

....

....

....

....

....

....

Score yourself on a scale of 1–10 based on your ability to innovate:

Circle One:

1   2   3   4   5   6   7   8   9   10

Indicator #5 Nuggets

Your challenges are just opportunities to create unique
solutions. Your business and relationships must embrace
Innovation to have the ability to grow.

If it works, break it down and systematize it;
If it sucks don't use it anymore!

THE ABILITY TO ADAPT...IMMEDIATELY

While we were growing up, my brother was the greatest at everything. He played every sport, but this lesson will come from his time on the grid-iron. Rob could catch a ball better than anyone that I had ever seen. I believe that this came from my Pops having us stand up against his pride and joy, a 1967 MGBGT,[43] while he fired the football at us. I was the baby, so I don't think he threw it at me as hard as he did at Rob. My Pops would tell us that if the ball hit the car, he was going to whoop us. My brother would have red arms from the pigskin slamming into him, but he would make sure that the football never touched my pop's prized possession. This created the theory in our family that if you touch it, you catch it. This was never as evident to me as when I witnessed my brother Rob dive head first into a rose bush just to catch a ball in a pick-up game in our front yard. It didn't matter the arena Rob was locked on. He would

---

43   http://www.thetruthaboutcars.com/2009/04/curbside-classic-1967-mgb-gt/

never let the ball hit the ground. All he wanted to do was be a receiver, but the only challenge was no one on his team had the ability to throw the ball to him. The quarterback position was open, and he had an arm that made most envy him. The only challenge was he wanted to have nothing to do with that position.

My brother was at a crossroads—whether to hold tight to his desire or practice his **ability to adapt immediately**. He chose the latter and went on to become one of the best quarterbacks that I had ever seen.

I applied this lesson just the other day when a woman wasn't happy with our service. Even though we are closed on Sundays, it was the only time that she had available. Myself and another teammate went to her house which exceeded her expectations and solidified a lifetime relationship. This relationship will take work throughout the years but is now built on a firm foundation.

The Story of How My Ability to Adapt Immediately Launched My Career

I was working in a salon in Memphis and one night, I had no guests. In walks a woman to get her hair done by one of the top stylists in our company. She had brought a friend and had her sit in the waiting area as was customary for guests who weren't getting their hair done. I had a flashback to earlier in the day when I was walking around the salon with the owner Mike. We walked by a massage room that was vacant, and he explained that there used to be a massage therapist there. When I looked into the room, I noticed a dusty massage chair and asked him what it was. He laughed and explained to me that they, as a company, used to give a complimentary "stress relief" treatment to all of their guests before they enjoyed their hair services. "Genius" I remember thinking!

Now back to the woman sitting in the waiting room. Did I mention that she was beautiful? Minor details, but the fact that I was 19 years old at that time and it was quite an emphasis. As I got closer, I was scrambling for a conversation starter and then it hit me, "Complimentary Stress Relief Treatment"! That was it. I reached out my hand and introduced myself. She quickly replied her name was Suzie. I instantly told her that as opposed to just waiting on her friend to get her hair done, I would love to blow dry and style her hair...wait for it ...and that I gave a "Complimentary Stress Relief Treatment" with every service. I offered to even do the style complimentary. I created a situation where she could not say **no**. She did throw me for a loop when she asked what the "Complimentary Stress Relief Treatment" was. I acted on my feet and told her I would be right back. I ran to the back of the salon into the abandoned massage room, grabbed the massage chair, dusted it off, and set it up. There were no face papers to be found, so I ran into the bathroom, grabbed two paper towels, folded them in half, and set them up as if that was the procedure all along. I went to the front and escorted Suzie to the massage chair, and she sat down on it not knowing that I had never used this contraption before. I started massaging her and as she responded, I adapted to it.

I tell you, I was making things up as I went. By the time it was done, she was relaxed and then I shampooed her head, and finished the service by blow dry styling her hair. Throughout the service, we talked about her interests. And I found out that she was a competition dancer on the 9-time National Champion University of Memphis Pom Squad! I continued to emphasize that I did a "Complimentary Stress Relief Treatment" with every service and that she should tell her friends. Suzie became my first evangelist and caused my business to explode. I went from 4 guests with no walk-in clients to being booked 8 weeks solid on the 45-minute mark, with a 45-person waiting list, in only 16 months. I believe that your ability to adapt immediately can be the difference between the ordinary and extraordinary.

I liken this process to a muscle much like faith. God builds us from faith to faith and glory to glory as long as we are open. This final indicator is more of a discipline to me that needs to be constantly worked on. The old cliché says *you must play to win* and *avoid playing not to lose*. This concept requires you to play loose, "To be like water my friend" as Bruce Lee would say. No rigid reaction or stance, just the ability to adapt to your environment, and the confidence in knowing that you will not lose yourself at the end of all of it.

Your success in life and business teeters on your ABILITY TO ADAPT IMMEDIATELY.

E G O

Ego is one of the quickest and most deadly killers of business and relationship. I have watched some of the greatest youngsters start out with the best of intention only to fall victim to a simple 3-letter word that can be easily avoided if we practice this discipline. When you adapt immediately, you realize that anyone can do the same. You also realize that the difference between the elite and the good is really splitting hairs. John Paul Dejoria[44] says, **"The difference between successful people and unsuccessful people is that successful people are willing to do things that unsuccessful people aren't willing to do!"** Bam! That was a NUGGET!

I love to put myself around young people because their ability to adapt will make your head spin. Nowadays, kids are doing what took me years to do in a matter of months, if not weeks. It keeps me in check and shows me that I need to work this muscle to stay sharp and relevant. Let's not mis-

---

44 http://www.businessinsider.in/The-difference-between-successful-people-and-unsuccessful-people-according-to-billionaire-John-Paul-DeJoria/articleshow/47031619.cms

take this with being trendy. That is another process altogether and will prove to be fleeting.

The ability to adapt immediately works best when it is in line with your core values. If you want to control your ego or better yet, strangle it into submission, work out this muscle that most are unaware of. Watch this…are you ready… When this muscle is strong, it will cause your ego to retreat. Understand that no matter whatever you accomplish or conquer, you will never arrive. Remember, you will only progress on your journey! There will always be a kid waiting in the shadows for you to blaze a trail, allowing them to know what is possible, and making your biggest accomplishment their starting line.

Your Reaction Time Will Determine Your Reward

Can you imagine if you would've been the first employee at Apple and had the foresight to just stay with the company! How about investing in Microsoft in the 80s! John Paul Dejoria spoke in his documentary "Good Fortune"[45] about an investor that he had lined up who was going to get 40–50% of Paul Mitchell[46] only to back out at the last minute! There are so many of these stories, and these are just a few, but do you see the lesson in all of this?

We used to live on base because my Pops was in the mili-

---

45 http://www.latimes.com/fashion/la-ig-john-paul-dejoria-good-fortune-20170703-htmlstory.html
46 https://en.wikipedia.org/wiki/Paul_Mitchell_(hairdresser)#Personal_life

tary. We shopped at the BX for school clothes, and although they were inexpensive, the clothes that we got were generally about a year behind the trend. I learned a valuable lesson in business from this experience.

NUGGET:

The price may be lower if you wait, but the value of your investment may not have as much upside.

In no way am I saying that you should be hasty in your decisions. Remember, this muscle is only valuable when you apply it ruthlessly with your core principle in mind. There is no replacement for people who believe in things from the beginning.

Sara Bryan was a name that I did not recognize on my schedule. It was my first week of working on my own and all of the guests were believers in what I was doing. This is why I focused on that name. For the life of me, I could not recall who it was. When the appointment time came, I met a young lady that would not only change my life but also have a profound effect on the hair industry as a whole. As I took care of her hair, she explained that she was a hairdresser herself. I nonchalantly mentioned that I would love to work with her if she was ever to move to Las Vegas. (She lived in Maui at the time and had flown in just to get her hair done.) Six weeks later, I received a message saying that she transferred her license, found an apartment, and was asking when could she start. I was blown away, and also intrigued by the audacity of this woman to move from paradise to the desert. I like "crazy" and that is what I saw in Sara from the early stages. Most called me "crazy" when I lost my job and started telling people that I was going to *revolutionize* our industry. They also called me crazy when I chose to be a hairdresser. I embrace "crazy." In fact, I have built my entire existence on it. So when I recognized this trait, I wanted to create a position for her even though I had nothing at the time. She started, committed, and has never looked back. She started with me at $5 an hour and elevated to 6 figures in 3½ years, increasing every year since. Now eleven years later, she is the VP of our company that includes five salons nationwide and employs nearly seventy people. She invested early, adapted herself to the circumstances, and now has a position that cannot be replaced.

The best way to keep your ego in check and ensure the highest return on your investment depends on your *ability to adapt immediately.*

I would like you to list out 5 places where your ego has hurt your growth.

....

....

....

....

....

Write down 3 instances where delay in adapting cost you dearly.

....

....

....

....

....

....

Finally, score yourself on a scale of 1–10 based on your actions (not intention) of your ability to adapt immediately:

Circle One:

1   2   3   4   5   6   7   8   9   10

INDICATOR #6 NUGGET

The price may be lower if you wait, but the value of your investment may not have as much upside.

FINAL WORDS

1 — Culture

2 — Vibe

3 — Process (Procedure)

4 — Productivity

5 — Innovation

6 — The Ability to Adapt Immediately

I get so excited as I write these words because they have life and legs not only in our company and family, but also in every person who comes in contact with these indicators.

I test this in every situation that arises now in my life. When things in your business or relationships start to break down or simply need an adjustment, revisit these 6 Indicators to get you back on track. We all know there are no magic Beans—only hard work and perspective can help you to improve in all that you do. Remember, anything you focus on will grow. If you want exponential growth, learn to celebrate the success of your team members publicly. Simple words and phrases that can change the way you look at your life. I have to admit that in the process of writing this book, I have had to take a look at all of these aspects in my life. At the end of each chapter, I have asked you to complete a couple of assignments and to score yourself on a scale of 1–10 on all of these indicators. I encourage you to do that right now with all six of them in your journal. We do this in every location at the end of the night and in whichever area we score low, we emphasize that area the next day. This process will cause you to be acutely aware of your environment and enable you to constantly make it better.

By no means is this a way to run your business on autopilot. Rather, you must be active in implementing these indicators, or they will be just words on a page. When you apply these using your unique personality and skill set, it will create an environment that is alive. Your distinctive signature will soon become evident, and that is something that no one can compete with.

This isn't just about another quick fix that promises to resolve all your business issues. This is about identifying your core values and taking the long road that will prove to be sustainable. My Pops always told me, "There is only one business in the world and one business only, and that is the people business. If you ever take the 'people' out of the business, you will have no business at all!" That is my last nugget to hopefully drive home the fact that these indicators are meant to enhance your emphasis on people, not to replace it. When you place people first, and you are guided by integrity-based indicators, your success is inevitable.

Now, you are not done when you close these pages. Rather, you have just embarked on a journey that will break you down only to build you into the person that you were purposed to be.

KELLY CARDENAS

Kelly Cardenas speaks all over the world
to various businesses and schools
helping people to realize their potential.

For all booking requests please contact:
booking@kellycardenas.com
or visit *kellycardenas.com*

CPSIA information can be obtained
at www.ICGtesting.com
Printed in the USA
LVOW03*0404100118
562477LV00001B/1/P